The Fabulous ONASSIS

1. Aristotle Onassis

The Fabulous ONASSIS
His Life and Loves

BY CHRISTIAN CAFARAKIS

With JACQUES HARVEY

Translated from the French by

JOHN MINAHAN

William Morrow & Company, Inc. New York 1972

French edition published by Productions de Paris—N.O.É., under the title *Le Fabuleux Onassis,* © 1971 by N.O.É.

PICTURE CREDITS
1–4; 8–11: United Press International Photos.
5–7; 12–18: Wide World Photos.

Printed in the United States of America.
Library of Congress Catalog Card Number 73-188186

2 3 4 5 75 74 73 72

Contents

Illustrations

(between pages 72 and 73)

The Fabulous ONASSIS

1 | The *Christina*

"By God, you'll *sink* it, you'll *sink* it, you'll *sink* this ship!"

The voice booming through the half-open door leading to the lounge could be heard all over the vessel and even reached my neophyte ears. I'd been aboard the *Christina,* the most famous yacht in the world, for all of ten minutes.

Three days before, when the yacht was anchored at Corfu, Mrs. Tina Onassis had recommended me for a job at first sight. Well, to tell the truth, she didn't exactly keel over in ecstasy and cry, "You're dynamite, you absolutely knock me out." Nothing like that. Actually, I'd taken the initiative when I saw the *Christina* anchored in the bay of my native island and I made sure I was right on the dock when Madame landed in the Chris-Craft. Scared to death, I stepped forward and asked her somewhat impulsively if she needed a sailor aboard who could also serve as a waiter.

She gave me a long look, then kindly advised me to go to the offices of Olympic Maritime in Athens and tell them she'd sent me. I didn't have to be asked twice.

I was a young man then, and one of my dreams was

about to come true: I was going to leave Greece and travel the world.

At Olympic Maritime, everything went very well, although rather strangely. As soon as I told the personnel director that I was sent by Mrs. Onassis, I was received with open arms, but then I was subjected to somewhat unusual questioning. For instance, they asked me if I knew how to dance. Surprised, I replied that I was sure the Onassises didn't intend me to be a nightclub entertainer. Somewhat embarrassed, my interviewer, a fat man with childlike round cheeks, informed me that everyone aboard the *Christina* had to know how to dance.

Then he wanted to know if I liked women, since apparently disciples of Castor and Pollux were not welcome on board. I had no trouble in answering that I was attracted by the fair sex, for which I was warmly congratulated. Luckily, too, I was able to answer that I spoke French. I was offered the job. The pay was a hundred dollars a month, take it or leave it. Naturally, even though I wasn't going to make my fortune, I accepted immediately.

Early the next day, I found myself aboard the *Christina,* hearing for the first time this incredibly angry voice shouting curses at some poor unseen audience.

A mechanic named Dragonas, who was standing next to me at the time, gazed resignedly at the ceiling. "Today, it's better to stay clear of Barbas," he told me. "He's in a foul temper."

Barbas in Greek means "uncle." I innocently asked which uncle he was talking about.

Dragonas stared at me as if I came from outer space. "*Which* Barbas? Barbas is the *boss,* you clown!"

I learned later that many people referred to Aristotle Onassis as Barbas behind his back, sort of a constant reminder that the man was infinitely rich and powerful and therefore considered something of a patriarch. If the Americans have Uncle Sam, the Greeks have Uncle Onassis.

I absorbed a lot of information very quickly that first day. The *Christina* had a crew of sixty—officers, sailors and miscellaneous staff—for the various specialized tasks, but no one really had a single well-defined job. For example, the first mate warned me right away that in addition to waiting on table, I'd also have to clean the dining room. With that, he promptly handed me a broom, pail and mop.

But to return to that thundering voice once again: after a solid half-hour, the shouting ceased rather abruptly and a tall, gangling man with a sad expression emerged from the lounge, carrying a toolbox under his heavily muscled arm. Obviously, he'd been the recipient of Onassis' tirade.

The man paused, glanced at us and slowly lit a cigarette. "As if I were going to sink his precious yacht," he said softly. "Big deal. Barbas finds me shining the copper section of the portholes with a very fine piece of emery paper rather than one of those household cleansers." He shrugged, smiled. "I bet if you asked him how long it'd take to rub the whole God-damn ship away by scrubbing the decks with extra-fine sandpaper, he'd *still* have the answer!"

He wandered off, bearing all the burdens of the

world on his shoulders, while I began sweeping my floor very lightly, hoping that if Barbas passed he wouldn't start by saying that my broom was as soft as steel wool. I kept telling myself that when you own a $6,000,000 yacht, you're entitled to a few little idiosyncrasies.

But after working almost ten years for Onassis I now understand how much he loves the *Christina.* When he comes aboard after a few days' absence, he always observes the same ritual. Accompanied by the captain, the first mate and the chief engineer, he makes a meticulous tour of inspection. Since he knows that the lounge and his cabin are always impeccable, he doesn't even bother with them. Instead, he visits the most unlikely places. With his finger or a white handkerchief, he searches for dust in remote corners and there's hell to pay if he finds any. On those occasions, there just aren't enough gods in Greek mythology to bear witness that everyone is conspiring against him. Sometimes, he's shouted so loud and long that he's actually lost his voice for several days.

I vividly remember one time when Onassis returned to the yacht, anchored near his villa at Glyfada, a suburb of Athens, after a ten-day stay in Paris. He decided he wanted to see the galleys, the engine room and the officers' cabins. Four of these cabins shared a single bathroom, which he also wanted to study. After careful inspection, his glance fell upon a tiny spot on the carpet behind the bidet. It so happened that the drainpipe had been dripping very slowly for several days. The cabin boy in charge of cleaning the area had asked one of the handymen to fix it. Unfortunately, the man forgot.

Onassis immediately summoned the cabin boy in question and remarked that, judging by the deposit of salt, the leak must have been there for at least two weeks. Because he hadn't called someone in to fix it, he was guilty of negligence. Onassis promptly gave the boy his notice, with orders to leave the ship the following morning.

There had been negligence, all right, but of course the cabin boy wasn't the guilty party. Still, rather than inform on a colleague, the lad accepted his dismissal without a word.

The story didn't end there, however, and what follows is a typical example of Onassis' most fundamental characteristic. He considers and reconsiders even the most minute and seemingly futile problems.

After dinner the same evening, he went out on the main deck and began pacing back and forth. Suddenly he returned to the lounge and sent for the boy he'd fired only a few hours earlier. This time he asked the young man *why* he hadn't reported the leak to anyone. Still not wanting to betray his friend the handyman (who, it turned out, was later traitorous enough to claim that no one had ever mentioned the matter to him), the boy said he'd simply forgotten. In Onassis' book, this was the worst crime of all.

"You *forgot?*" he said, over and over again, as he always does when he's outraged. "Do *I* ever forget to fulfill my responsibilities to *you?*"

Gradually his anger subsided, and in a kind voice he told the boy to go to bed; he would discuss the matter in the morning. Ten minutes later, the handyman was sent on his way. No one had told on him, but Onassis guessed the truth. Although the incident is trivial in itself, I think it provides at least an insight into one of the most significant aspects of the man's personality.

Now let me give you some facts and figures about the *Christina*, things you don't usually read in the press. The yacht was formerly a 1,800-ton Royal Canadian frigate, 325 feet in length. It was completely refurbished three times in Hamburg before it met Onassis' exacting specifications. The bottom of the swimming pool is designed in delicate blue-and-white mosaics and can be raised electrically to become a dance floor. The next deck has nine guest cabins, named after various Greek islands. Onassis has an apartment of his own, consisting of an office, bedroom and semicircular bathroom. The latter has always intrigued me, not because of the famous silver and gold fixtures, but because of the door, which is actually a one-way mirror. I've never understood exactly why Onassis feels the need to see what goes on in his bedroom when he's in the bathroom. He certainly didn't have it installed to spy on the chambermaids or any other members of the staff who might wander in there, since everyone aboard knew about the "magic mirror."

The only conclusion that makes any sense to me is that Onassis wanted to be able to see—from wherever he was in the apartment—the precious icons and the painting by El Greco that adorn the wall of his cabin.

In a very real sense, the *Christina* is something of a floating museum. In the lounge, there's another El Greco, a Gauguin and a Pissarro. The dining room has a Vermeer and an interesting collection of paintings representing the four seasons. Tina and her two children, Alexandre and Christina, were the models for Autumn,

Winter and Spring, while Summer was represented by a young lady in a swimsuit, lying on a beach with the casino of Monte Carlo in the distance.

Of course, everywhere you look are objets d'art. An amethyst Buddha, apparently one of three of its kind in the world, is said to be worth a fortune in itself. Onassis also has an outstanding collection of eighteenth-century ivory boats. Lesser valuables are all over: little gold tobacco boxes, pewter platters, a jug adorned with the bust of Winston Churchill, the Steinway used by Maria Callas for over ten years, a slot machine from Monte Carlo, an electric guitar for John-John Kennedy's use.

Perhaps Onassis' most treasured objects, in a symbolic sense anyway, are the magnificent bar and stools decorated with whales' teeth. One day an officer and a group of sailors told me their history. In March, 1956, a part of the Onassis fleet was in the Arctic Sea hunting whales. The fleet consisted of sixteen whaling vessels, a special "factory" ship where the whales were actually butchered and stored and a tanker providing fuel for the others. These vessels were flying the Liberian flag, as do all of Onassis' fleet, including the *Christina.* The expedition was headed by a former naval admiral who had long been in Onassis' service.

When the legal quota of whales had been killed, the fleet headed back to Rotterdam, a twelve-day trip. But when they reached the middle of the Atlantic, the admiral found himself in the midst of an enormous school of whales, a dream come true for any whaler. The admiral knew only too well that he had to ignore this, but he couldn't resist sending Onassis a cable to inform him of the tempting situation. The reply came back: "EMPTY TANKER FUEL, FILL CISTERNS WITH WHALE OIL."

Unfortunately, one of the ships harbored some spies for a rival company, who managed to alert the international authorities. Onassis was not without his own sources of information, heard of the betrayal, realized how much an investigation would cost him, but knew only three days were left to find a solution before the scheduled arrival in Holland.

By the time the fleet reached Rotterdam, every last ship was flying a Japanese flag. Onassis had sold his vessels to a Japanese firm that had been after him to sell for a long time. When the authorities discovered the extra whale oil, the Japanese truthfully disclaimed any knowledge of the matter and the whole affair was allowed to drop.

A few days later, Onassis ordered a quantity of whales' teeth shipped to him in Greece to decorate his bar, as a souvenir of the incident which, instead of costing him a fortune, resulted in several million dollars' profit.

To conclude my description of the *Christina,* I should mention that the galleys are completely electric, while the hold is equipped with refrigerators and cold-storage rooms capable of holding several tons of supplies. Safety has been given paramount consideration: the hydroplane is always fueled and ready to go at a moment's notice; there are six lifeboats on the upper deck, four Chris-Craft and two smaller vessels.

On a good day, the *Christina* looks like a sumptuous California villa, but in turbulent weather, it's a different story altogether. She's moody, sluggish and awkward enough to worry the most seasoned sailor. Probably because he reasoned that the vibrations of a powerful motor would damage his paintings and objets d'art, Onassis decided to retain the *Christina*'s original steam engines, with the result that her top speed is only fourteen knots. Worse still, another deck was added, making the vessel proportionately too high for its length. Consequently, in rough weather, the *Christina* is rather like a sailor without his sea legs.

Actually, we were lucky enough to avoid most bad storms, but I do remember one which I'm certain no one aboard will ever be able to forget. It was May, 1958, and Onassis had several guests (among them Gregory Peck and Greta Garbo), as well as his sister and brother-in-law, the Garoufalideses, Tina, the children and their nurse. We were in the Strait of Messina headed toward Capri, where we planned to anchor for a few days. The sea was calm, the sun shining brilliantly and everyone was in such a good mood that Onassis ordered Louis, the barman, to put on an album of Spanish music.

Gregory Peck, who'd been lying indolently in the sun, sprang to his feet, grabbed the red tablecloth that Onassis had just picked up, and immediately started playing the toreador. Onassis became the bull, lowering his head menacingly, while everyone else clapped their hands to the music, entering into the spirit of the game.

Onassis had already missed his quarry several times and it was almost time for "the moment of truth," when Captain Schlatermund appeared with a very worried expression. Without the slightest hesitation, he went to Onassis and asked to speak to him privately. We all knew that if Schlatermund dared to interrupt the boss like that, there must be serious trouble.

In fact, the *Christina* was headed straight into a violent storm. Everything happened so quickly, it was difficult to believe. In less than forty-five minutes, the ship began to roll ominously and in no time at all it became unbearable; at times we literally couldn't tell which end was up. Somehow Onassis managed (God knows how!) to get down to the engine room. Drenched and shaken badly, he burst into the room shouting, trying to be heard over the tremendous noise, asking Kimon, the chief engineer, if the ship was going to make it. Kimon remembers himself flabbergasted; he expected the engines—running at full force—to explode at any minute and believed his last hour had come.

"God damn it, will she make it!" Onassis kept shouting.

"I don't know!" Kimon kept saying. "Christ, I just don't know!"

At the very height of the storm, the *Christina* rolled over a full twenty-seven degrees, which meant in effect that the slightest incorrect maneuver or any appreciably higher wave could easily have sent us to the bottom. Everyone was in a state of absolute panic. Some of the sailors were convinced that Onassis, Tina and the children were going to abandon them by taking the hydroplane to safety, an utterly ridiculous idea considering how impossible it would have been to launch anything at all in that sea.

All this time the guests were sweating it out below, terrified, all violently ill, tossed around their cabins like dice in a cup.

The storm lasted sixteen hours. Finally, at about eight o'clock in the morning, the sea calmed somewhat and we were able to see Capri in the distance. The *Christina* entered the harbor in all her former glory, to the admiration of hundreds of tourists gathered at the docks, but no one could understand why the guests were in such a tremendous hurry to get off and seemed so happy at the sight of solid ground.

Later Onassis admitted that for the first time in his life he had been afraid of the sea. In fact, he had been sure that the vessel was going to split in two. Naturally, all of us had been aware that the weak engines and added height of the ship constituted a very real danger. What's more, the experts who came to inspect the *Christina* a few days later, in Monte Carlo, declared that the stabilizers had been incorrectly adjusted by a British firm some time before, when the ship was in Southampton. Onassis spent a total of $75,000 to have the whole job redone. Still, in later years, there were certain cruises when many of his guests would have paid any amount of money to be safely at home, rather than on the *Christina.*

My first evening aboard, I waited on table as I'd been hired to do, trying to learn the habits and idiosyncrasies of my new boss as quickly as possible. This was no small task. My first run-in with him was over the serving of an orange. Onassis is very proud of his oranges, which come from his own garden in Glyfada. Every week an Olympic Airways plane brings him several crates, no matter where he happens to be in the world at the time.

I remember it was about 11 P.M. when Onassis saw

me on deck and asked for an orange. It was my first private assignment for him and I headed happily for the galley, picked up the best orange I could find and placed it on a plate. Proud that the whole operation hadn't taken more than a couple of minutes, I dashed back to present my offering. Onassis took the plate, glanced at the orange, frowned at me (standing at attention), then started his tirade. I listened, understanding very little of what he was shouting, until I was able to distinguish the word *knife*. My first job for the boss, and I blew it!

In retrospect, I can understand that *anyone* in his place would lose his temper more than once a day aboard the *Christina* or on Onassis' island of Skorpios, in the Ionian Sea, because the service was in fact deplorable most of the time. Perhaps this was owing in part to Tina, who was "living in a cloud," as her husband used to say. She didn't exercise her authority in supervising the servants at all, and the consequences were quite predictable. Onassis, too, could be lax with the help, especially with one of his favorites. I remember a story about a crewman that will demonstrate the point.

One day when we were anchored in Monte Carlo, Tina received a phone call from the woman who regularly supplied flowers for the yacht. She was in some kind of trouble and urgently needed the three thousand dollars that was owed to her. (Flowers for the *Christina*, which Tina liked to have everywhere, from bathroom to galley, came to about one hundred dollars per day.) Tina, who was kindness personified, immediately gave the money to the crewman, in cash, to deliver to the woman right away. He set off at noon, but still hadn't returned by five o'clock, although the errand shouldn't have taken more than half an hour.

Of course, the explanation was simple. While Onassis was helping himself to his favorite aperitif, ouzo, and beginning to worry about what could've happened to him, the man was at the casino, in the process of losing the last few dollars of the florist's money. Flat broke, he returned sadly and confessed his sins.

In spite of this, it was a full six months before the crewman finally left Onassis' service, not that Tina didn't plead daily with her husband to get rid of him. In the meantime, the crewman managed to completely demolish two Ferraris that Onassis lent him. Not one, but *two*! The fact of the matter was simply that the boss just didn't want to fire him. He liked him in spite of his innumerable transgressions. So Tina was forced to wait patiently to free herself of this man, whom she considered a distinct liability. Her chance came at the beginning of 1958, when Onassis was away on a business trip in Mexico.

Tina summoned the crewman, instructing him to pay her dressmaker in Cannes. In my opinion, she consciously arranged a trap, because she gave him cash once again, instead of a check. This time, he managed to avoid the casino in Monte Carlo, but fell prey to the Palais de la Mediterranée in Nice. He played non-stop till two in the morning. I don't know exactly how much cash he started with, but apparently by midnight he was rich, ready to buy the *Christina* if Lady Luck didn't desert him. Which, of course, she did at exactly 12:30 A.M. By two o'clock he was simply the crewman again—the man Tina was calmly waiting to fire.

But to continue about the service in general, once

I asked the Greek cook how much food and drink we were in the habit of taking on an average two-week cruise. I'd long been struck by the enormous quantity of supplies that were brought aboard each week. The cook estimated the following figures: at least ten whole veal roasts, ten baby pigs, ten lambs, six roasts of beef and about two hundred chickens. (It was customary to have chicken every Sunday on the *Christina.*) As for fish, he estimated about five hundred pounds, plus around fifty lobsters and several eels for good measure.

The one thing we never needed to take along was bread. Until 1961, it always arrived by plane. It seems that one day while eating in a Paris restaurant, Onassis fell in love with the bread regularly served there. Straightaway, he obtained the name of the baker, who was located on the corner of Avenue Victor Hugo and rue des Belles-Feuilles. When he was in Paris, all Onassis had to do was send his chauffeur Rozas to buy the bread; but since he was seldom there, he devised a complicated system to fly it in fresh. Every day, Rozas would buy the precious bread, speed it to Orly Airport and put it on the Olympic flight that came closest to where Onassis was at the time. When we were at sea, George Kuris, the hydroplane pilot, would pick it up at the nearest airport.

In 1961, Maria Callas, who'd been with Onassis for two years by that time, couldn't help suggesting that it would be much more economical to send the cook, Clément Miral, to Paris to learn how to bake the special bread. From that time on, Miral held the new position of chief cook and baker until Jackie Onassis discovered that the sister of Nikos (the sole restaurant owner on the island of Lefkas, opposite Skorpios) made a certain bread that was absolutely "darling-darling."

So now, once again, the bread is brought in by plane, despite the extra inconvenience and cost. One sailor on the *Christina* estimated that on certain days the bread must cost at least two hundred dollars. The nearest airport to Lefkas is Corfu, which means that a ship or a plane must first make the round trip to the airport; then the bread must be sent to Athens, where it can be put aboard an international flight, which might be bound for New York, just as well as Paris or London. If one is accustomed to paying little for a loaf of bread, this does seem a bit extravagant. But for Onassis, it's a minor detail. He simply wants his family and friends to have what they enjoy most. Which is not exactly the rule when it comes to his personnel.

Granted, the *Christina* has many comforts for the crew that you wouldn't find on just any pleasure ship. For instance, all the cabins for guests and crew alike are comfortably air-conditioned. But in all honesty, despite the mountains of food and drink purchased for the yacht, the crew eats rather poorly. And if you have the misfortune of being Greek, you can't even get a drink! The crew dining room is separated into two sections by a large cream-colored screen; Greeks eat on one side, non-Greeks on the other. When I asked the reason for this, I found that it was because of the wine. Onassis more or less observes a law of the Greek Merchant Marine that forbids sailors to be given wine. Therefore, we were allowed only a bottle of beer every Saturday and Sunday, while the French and German sailors were each allotted a half-bottle of wine per meal. Needless to say, this created fierce jealousies among us, but nothing was ever changed, despite the numerous petitions we sent to the boss via an officer.

The Greek Merchant Marine was also responsible for our daily menus, which were the same week after week, year after year. We always knew that on Monday we'd have fish, Tuesday sausages, and so on. This was not only monotonous, but quite frustrating, especially when we watched the chefs prepare *haute cuisine* meals for the family and guests.

But to be honest about it, this routine didn't really bother me that much, since my ambition at the time was not to be a gourmet but to do my job as well as I could in order to get a more interesting job. In the meantime, I used my free time to explore the ship, which was how I happened to go down and visit Joseph and his wife, the couple who did the laundry and dry cleaning.

We used to call them "the groundhogs," because they spent their entire time buried under huge piles of laundry, deep down in the heart of the ship; we saw them only at mealtimes. When I went down to chat with them, they were much too busy to reply with anything more than a grunt or an occasional monosyllable. I was about to leave when I happened to stumble over a pile of shirts next to the door, and I heard the unmistakable sound of cloth tearing. I turned around, expecting to face a very annoyed Joseph, but to my great surprise he didn't seem at all upset.

"Christ," I said. "I think I've torn one of the boss's shirts."

Joseph smiled. "My dear fellow, down here we wouldn't know if the boss even *wears* shirts!"

Sadly, it wasn't the boss's shirts I'd stepped on, but the professional pride of that hard-working couple. They admitted that the boss only gave them his underwear, socks and suits to clean.

I was perplexed because I knew that Onassis sometimes changed his shirt as often as six times a day. As a parting remark, Joseph's wife suggested that perhaps *Tina* washed her husband's shirts. Amusing idea.

The executive secretary for the *Christina* finally solved the "mystery" by telling me that Onassis' shirts were flown out once a week to a special laundry in Athens, the only one he tolerated. Whether he's in Paris, New York or aboard ship, his shirts are always done in Greece. Of course, transportation is rather difficult, because the shirts must not be folded, but placed on hangers! The most ironic aspect of this whole situation, which could run into a great deal of money for anyone who didn't own an international airline, is that Onassis absolutely refuses to give a shirt away until it's virtually in rags, long after the collar and cuffs have been redone several times.

Aside from this peculiarity, Onassis can't really be accused of being a vain man. His wardrobe consists of a dozen or so dinner jackets and maybe fifty suits, all of which are either dark blue or dark gray. In fact, Hélène, his maid in Paris, says he hardly needs that number, because he prefers to wear the same suit day after day and only requires that it be freshly pressed for him each morning.

When he's on vacation in Greece, on the island or the yacht, he dresses casually in shorts that come down to his knees and cotton T-shirts that are so decrepit that he needn't worry about anyone stealing *them*! In fact, it was owing to this rather shabby costume that he had an interesting adventure in Thessalonica in 1964.

The ship was anchored in the bay and Onassis, accompanied by three sailors, decided to go ashore to discuss the unloading of some merchandise. In addition to his regular outfit, he was wearing an old beret that once had been white but was then quite yellowed with age.

When Onassis and the sailors landed, they were immediately hailed by the dock workers, who were always anxious to find out all about the *Christina* and its famous owner. They obviously didn't recognize him and started right in by asking: "Is the old bastard still as cheap as he used to be?" They continued with all manner of crude speculations about his private life, while Onassis listened patiently. The remarks became considerably more vulgar as time went on. Meanwhile, the sailors desperately tried to indicate who was in their presence, to no avail. When there was nothing left for the workers to say, Onassis' only comment was, "At least I know one place where I'm well liked."

He calmly got back aboard the Chris-Craft, leaving the horror-stricken men nervously twisting their caps —which they'd somewhat belatedly had the courtesy to snatch from their heads.

2 | Monte Carlo

Certainly nothing like that could've happened in Monte Carlo. Onassis was so well liked there that some people unofficially renamed the principality "Monte Greco" soon after he'd more or less taken it over, and I think most people who lived there for a long time knew Onassis by sight. Thanks to his arrival, they still didn't have to pay taxes, as was threatened early in the 1950s when the affairs of the realm were going very badly.

Certain people maintain it was simply by chance that Onassis became a kind of second ruler in Monte Carlo. Clearly, in 1952, he had no plans for becoming the major stockholder of a company that operated the casino, some nightclubs, a beach, a bowling alley and five hotels. At that time, Onassis was simply looking around for a place to set up his offices in a country where he wouldn't be bothered by internal revenue. Since he was used to the Riviera and adored the sea (as does any Greek worth his salt), he asked his aides to find a large building suitable to his needs. They suggested the old Winter Sporting Club behind the Hotel de Paris in Monte Carlo. The ancient building belonged to the Société des Bains de Mer, a company which was just on the verge of collapse because tourists and gamblers were no longer coming to the resort. When the directors found out that Onassis wanted to move there, they leaped at the opportunity to offer him a deal: he could move into the Winter Sporting Club and have his official residence in Monte Carlo; at the same time, he would become the major stockholder in their company.

Surprisingly enough, Onassis burst out laughing at this proposition. It turns out that some thirty years before, on his way to Argentina in 1923, he'd taken a freighter from Genoa which stopped first at Marseilles. The ship naturally passed by Monte Carlo, the meeting place of kings and millionaires, and Onassis remarked to a Greek friend, his companion in poverty, "See that little corner of paradise? Some day I, too, will have a house there." Now, for the paltry sum of only $1,000,000, the entire country was being laid at his feet.

Onassis promised Prince Rainier to do everything in his power to raise Monte Carlo to its former glory, but only after he'd taken time to set up his offices in the sporting club. Actually, only a single year was needed for his name to attract rich tourists.

In time, Onassis became great friends with Prince and Princess Rainier. People still remember the fabulous parties he used to give for them aboard the *Christina,* which was anchored near their own yacht. I was present at one of the most sumptuous of these gala evenings.

One morning the first mate, Andriatos, assembled the entire crew, and informed us that if we were interested in keeping our jobs, the ship had to be as shiny as a new penny for the prince and princess. That night they were to attend a reception for over sixty people. We whisked out our white paint, varnish, soap, brushes, brooms and aprons to obey the captain's order. Andriatos warned a few of us that the boss would make an inspection around six o'clock that evening. Unfortunately, my corridor was right in the path of all the deliveries and extra activities caused by the coming festivities. I couldn't remove the grease spots and cigarette ashes fast enough. At 5:30 P.M., when the final delivery of food for the party was made, I was in despair. The men were too busy paying attention to their precious burdens to consider the spotlessness of my floor. The last straw was when a mechanic, who had run out of cigarettes, took the staircase leading into my corridor without observing the rule of changing his shoes first. He had just completed a grimy trail when Onassis arrived, accompanied by the captain. They both stopped dead in their tracks when they saw my corridor. After carefully examining the whole area, Onassis stood right in front of me so I'd be sure to hear his opinion of my cleaning methods.

Exasperated beyond control, I completely forgot who I was addressing: "You just listen to me!" I shouted as loud as I could. "About forty employees pass through this miserable corridor every minute, not to mention delivery men and mechanics who forget to change their shoes! If you multiply this by sixty minutes, and that again by two, since as far as we know there are no one-legged men on this ship, you'll discover that every hour about four thousand eight hundred feet pass over an area of linoleum no bigger than twenty square yards! There's no conceivable way this corridor can rival the purity of your lounge!"

Throughout, Onassis listened to me, nodding his head with a studied air of concentration. When I finished, he turned to the captain and said, "Schlatermund, all my problems are solved. We seem to have an electronic computer on board!" He walked away, shaking his head as if he'd just made a priceless discovery; I stood leaning on my mop, dumbfounded that I hadn't been banished forever from the Onassis kingdom.

Finally everything was ready, including my corridor. The boat was ablaze with light, flowers bloomed everywhere and the swimming pool had been transformed into a Roman fountain, with jets of water rising in graceful arcs glowing with all the colors of the rainbow. The guests dined to the music of a French orchestra, while below in the cabins, three other musical groups that Onassis had flown in from Athens, Madrid and Mexico awaited their turn to play dance music.

Although many people took advantage of this splendid occasion to put on everything in their jewel boxes, Princess Grace appeared with almost no jewelry at all, wearing a simple pink satin evening gown that accentuated her beauty. Tina Onassis, in beige, was the only one who rivaled the princess in elegance. All the men, of course, wore dinner jackets, including King Farouk who, incidentally, had an adventure that evening that could have been disastrous.

It must have been 11:30 P.M. when Farouk got up from his armchair to look for a dance partner. He headed across the packed floor toward a young woman leaning on the railing, admiring the brilliantly lighted port. But as he maneuvered through the dancers in the midst of a fast number, the king managed to drop his revolver, which he always carried tucked into the belt of his trousers. Since his rank naturally prevented him from bending down to pick it up, the gun was soon being kicked all over the floor by the unsuspecting dancers. Frantic, he cornered one of the waiters, who happened to be a good friend of mine, and begged him to retrieve the weapon as discreetly as possible. Accordingly, my friend grabbed a tray with a few empty glasses and started to wend his way in and out of the couples in search of the gun. After a few tense minutes, he finally spotted it, let his napkin fall adroitly over it and thus presented the gun to his majesty. I later found out that the king never used a bodyguard and that he was considered one of the best shots in his country.

At midnight, Onassis organized a show of fireworks that lasted at least twenty minutes, followed by an exhibition by two water-skiers, who performed acrobatics around the ship at about fifty miles an hour, holding lights in their hands. The party was finally over at 4 A.M., and had cost $20,000.

The next day, the royal couple presented Onassis with a special white, blue and yellow parrot in a golden cage. It was named Peau de Vache. We used to call it "Ari's ara [parrot]."

The parrot immediately made itself at home on the *Christina* and we taught it a few tricks: how to whistle at girls on the dock, and to imitate the pop of a champagne cork, which wasn't very difficult considering the amount of champagne consumed during an average cruise. The only problem with Peau de Vache was that he didn't like men. He took every opportunity to peck at all of us, including Onassis, until the famous day when the millionaire saved the bird's life.

One morning when the boat was anchored at Skorpios, Peau de Vache suddenly panicked, took off, and in his confusion flew straight at a closed porthole. The shock knocked him out cold and he fell into the sea. Onassis, having witnessed the whole scene, immediately dove into the water and brought the bedraggled bird back on board. From that day on, Peau de Vache swore an eternal love for his savior and there was never any question of his biting Onassis again. A few years later, Maria Callas had Peau de Vache given to the family of one of the crew members because she thought he started the first number in his repertory just a little too early in the morning.

One of the first things I discovered when I started to work for the Onassises was that they were not a very devoted couple. Not a day passed when we didn't hear some story or other to do with Tina or the children, and by 1957 their marriage was plainly on the verge of breaking up. This seemed particularly sad since their courtship and romance was unusual and extremely touching.

To begin with, I want to point out that Onassis didn't need to become the son-in-law of Stavros Livanos, millionaire shipping magnate, for reasons of money or influence. On April 17, 1943, when he entered the lobby of the Plaza in New York and met Tina for the first time, he was thirty-seven years old and already a wealthy man, with a bank account of several million dollars. Although this was the third meeting between the two men, it was the first time Onassis met either of his two daughters, and as luck would have it, he fell in love with the youngest one, Tina, who was only fourteen years old at the time.

During the first month after this meeting, Onassis sent so many flowers and presents to the girl that Livanos finally summoned the impetuous Greek to tell him that his daughter Tina was just too young to be courted, much less married. Onassis completely agreed and said he'd wait. Even when Livanos, who considered this young man a good match, suggested that he could marry his eldest daughter, Onassis only repeated that he would wait. This he did for nearly three years, during which time he never missed an opportunity to write or visit the woman of his choice. Finally, in December, 1946, Tina Livanos became Tina Onassis, a name which was then well known only to a few international bankers.

By the eleventh year of their marriage, however, all romance and understanding had vanished and they lived under the same roof like two strangers, every so often making an attempt to appear united in front of their guests. On most evenings when there were no guests aboard, Tina would take her black Ford and go off to do the rounds of the nightclubs with friends, coming back very late at night.

One time I heard Tina confess to a friend that her husband's business didn't leave them very much time with each other. Nevertheless, I think that even a short while before their divorce, she was still in love with her husband; yet at age twenty-eight she couldn't bear living by herself for such long periods. I learned of an incident that occurred in August, 1958.

As usual, Tina had been out and came in around 2 A.M. to find her husband with his best friend Maris Embiricos, who had come aboard with two French girls, Caroline and Michele. At the sight of these two intruders, Tina simply put down her purse, grabbed both girls by the hair and literally catapulted them out onto the dock, while screaming that they need never set foot in her living room again. Onassis, at first stunned, finally ended up laughing at the whole thing, remarking to his friend that he'd married a veritable tigress.

In general, the couple never resorted to physical violence, although they made up for it by not hesitating to say what they thought of each other. That night, for instance, after Embiricos left, Tina gave her husband a piece of her mind before retreating to a special cabin of her own, which was reserved for such occasions.

When she wasn't living on the *Christina,* Tina lived in the Château de la Croé, in Cap d'Antibes. It had once been owned by King Leopold and later by the Duke of Windsor. The rent was so high that the owner, Lady Barbara Burton, suggested that Onassis buy it. He replied somewhat condescendingly that he took no interest in houses; he preferred to invest his money in ships rather than old stones. Much later, Greek shipping millionaire Stavros Niarchos, who married Tina's sister Eugenia, bought the château.

When Tina wasn't planning a party or traveling about shopping either in Paris, London or New York, her favorite pastime was water-skiing. She would set off for hours on end behind a Chris-Craft driven by her skilled pilot, Spiros Trilivas. But of course all her money didn't prevent her from being ultimately bored by this monotonous life. She didn't even have the satisfaction of bringing up her two children, since they had an American nurse (logically nicknamed "Miss Nursy") who took total responsibility for them.

Of course, Onassis also amused himself, usually with his favorite companion, Embiricos. This extremely rich Greek shipping magnate (who died in 1968 at the age of ninety-six) once spent a year and a half in an Athenian prison because the Germans found out he was supplying provisions for English submarines from his island Petalius. As far as the employees of the *Christina* were concerned, Embiricos had only one fault. He kept harping at Onassis that we were overpaid. "And what's more," he usually added, "you let yourself be robbed as if you ran an open market." This latter observation was certainly true.

In fact, the *Christina* was the center of intense pilferage; with the exception of works of art, almost everything else disappeared. One day, Onassis couldn't even put the hydroplane in the water because there was no fuel left, either in the plane itself or in the reserve tanks located on deck. Whiskey, champagne and a wide variety of rare liqueurs, as well as food, were taken by the crew from the hold of the ship and resold either to individuals or to shopkeepers—at unbeatable prices, of course. Even today, one can save a good deal of money by buying Dom Perignon on the island of Lefkas. This island, for some mysterious reason, has become renowned for its quality champagnes; the *Christina* still anchors there nine months a year.

In general, supplies of salmon, crab, lobster and shrimp were subject to inexplicable losses. I once met a man who'd bought a raincoat three sizes too big in order to hide the daily spoils collected from the ship. The only delicacy that wasn't popular with the help or their clients was white rat, although it seems that prepared with white wine and onions, it's delicious.

Onassis paid absolutely no attention to the warnings of Embiricos until the day when the two of them searched the garbage. I'll never forget that evening. We were anchored in Piraeus, the port of Athens, and I was coming back to the *Christina* around midnight with my friend Nicolas Ecaterinis, who was first mate on Embiricos' yacht, the *Doudouna.* We caught sight of our two employers scrutinizing the garbage cans, which were left out on the dock, and immediately hid ourselves to see what would happen. We couldn't hear what the two were saying, but Onassis, who as usual was in his shirtsleeves, emptied out the contents of one can after another while Embiricos made astonished remarks. After they finished and Onassis was accompanying his friend back to the *Doudouna,* I hastily said good-bye to Nicolas and slipped back onto the *Christina,* sensing an evil wind was about to blow and that there would be hell to pay. I wasn't too far wrong.

At two o'clock in the morning, we were all awakened and told to assemble in the dining room. Onassis was there, hands behind his back, walking up and down, studying each of us with his piercing eyes. He then let go with all his fury: "You're nothing more than a bunch of *crooks!* There are millions of starving people all over the world, and you throw anything and everything into the *garbage!* You'll soon see what kind of 'garbage' *you'll* have to eat from now on!" (I remember thinking of the white rats.)

He went over exactly what he'd found: two silver

forks, some enormous cuts of meat that must have been an unauthorized extra for the kitchen boys, pounds of leftover lentils from our midday meal and masses of fresh bread. Of course, even if most of us had nothing to do with the galley, Onassis was still justified in scolding us all. The staff prepared the menus he planned, but sometimes as much as *tripled* the quantity, which accounted for the terrific waste found in the garbage cans. We were informed that things were going to be a lot stricter for us.

The first person to suffer under this new regime was the boss's own cousin Agasian. Only two days after this incident, Onassis happened to come down to the galley to get some olives for cocktails. In general, he never bothered to check on what the cooks were making for dinner, but that day was an exception. He lifted the cover of the big pot on the main stove, dipped a large wooden spoon into it, and came up with a mixture of rice, meat and vegetables that was a far cry from anything on the menu for that day. The Greek cook turned three shades of red when Onassis asked him what the dish was for and finally had to reply that it was for Agasian. "And what does Agasian think he's going to do with it?" There was absolutely no answer to this (Agasian never came on board the *Christina*, since he was employed in the office of Olympic Maritime). Finally, at the end of his tether, Onassis forced the cook to confess that Agasian had ordered him to prepare a huge quantity of food twice a day to feed his *Great Dane!* Beside himself with rage at this new evidence of fraud, Onassis immediately left the yacht for Olympic Maritime and fired Agasian on the spot.

It seems to me that all this cheating was particularly

shameful because Onassis never neglected even his distant relatives, not to mention Greek people in general if they were in need. Every day he receives hundreds of letters asking for help and it's a rare case when he doesn't comply. In addition, every morning before he goes out he remembers to take along a pocketful of one-hundred-dollar bills for those people who stop him in the street with: "Mr. Onassis, I haven't eaten"; "Mr. Onassis, I have no work"; "Mr. Onassis, I want to go home to Greece." The man is always ready to listen to these demands and never refuses a small sum, anywhere from twenty dollars to one hundred dollars.

Naturally, if Onassis comes to the rescue of strangers, he's even more generous with his own employees. If someone needs money to build a house or a member of his family is sick, he immediately advances the money, which the employee pays back in installments taken from his monthly wage. More often than not, after several payments, Onassis will cancel the debt altogether.

Among the many people who've benefited from being in the service of this man, I'm reminded of George and Hélène, who have taken care of Onassis in his Paris apartment for over twenty years. One day in the spring of 1955, they asked for two weeks' vacation to get married in Greece. Onassis told them not to worry, that he'd take care of everything. They certainly weren't prepared for what eventually happened, and at first were a little disappointed, suspecting that their employer was going to arrange a Paris wedding so he wouldn't have to do without them for so long.

At that time, Onassis didn't own the island of Skorpios, so he went directly to his friend Embiricos, told him about his servants' decision and asked if he could celebrate the wedding on Petalius, since he wanted to have a big party. Embiricos agreed, but pointed out that it was going to cost a great deal of money.

It took Onassis quite a while to prepare for this wedding. He wanted, for example, to anchor the *Christina* at the island, but the bay wasn't deep enough. To dredge out the harbor took three months and cost at least $100,000. Meanwhile, George and Hélène had been kept totally in the dark about these preparations and, not daring to remind their employer, were depressed that he'd apparently forgotten them. Finally, Onassis told them that everything was ready: the wedding was set for July 18. George and Hélène embarked on the *Christina* from Monte Carlo. Onassis was the witness for George, and Embiricos for Hélène.

The celebration lasted three whole days and nights. Onassis had several Greek orchestras brought over from Athens and ten cooks were in charge of roasting lamb, fish and lobster. Since all the employees of the *Christina* were invited, everybody danced and had fun together regardless of social station. I've never heard about any king or millionaire going to so much trouble and expense on behalf of his servants.

Probably because he was so generous as a rule, Onassis wanted us to know how disappointed he was in our deceitful behavior, and that he would be less easy on us in the future. The first thing he did was to choose a spy among us. His choice was Achilles, the ship's carpenter, who'd been completely devoted to Onassis for years.

Achilles was the youngest of seventeen children from a poor family. By trade a carpenter, he could only find work as a stevedore in Piraeus where, in 1955, he heard of Onassis' generosity and kindness to his countrymen. He wasn't exactly sure just how to make contact with the famous millionaire, since he suspected a letter would get mixed in with several hundred others and be neglected.

Then he had the bright idea of supplying a young lady friend of his with some pink stationery. He asked her to write Onassis describing the desperate situation of her Greek friend. He sprinkled the epistle liberally with perfume, had her write PERSONAL in large letters on the front, and sent it off to Olympic Maritime in London. The English secretary reacted according to plan. Not daring to open the envelope, she passed it on directly to her boss. Onassis, amused and impressed by this ruse, hired the carpenter at once.

Achilles made a daily report to Onassis, but there was very little material at first, since we all were afraid of following the same path as Agasian. (Onassis went so far as to observe our goings and comings with binoculars from Olympic Maritime across the way, while Embiricos volunteered to do the same from his yacht.) We even began to think that our good behavior was going to earn us a little peace, when yet another scandal broke out concerning a certain German girl and Onassis' sky-blue Austin.

Peter, one of the sailors, decided to "borrow" the adorable little Austin, because he had a date with a young girl from Munich he'd met the night before at the Tip Top Bar in Monte Carlo. Peter was a handsome English fellow around thirty years old, and although he was only a simple mechanic, he'd told her he was the first mate of the *Christina.* To supply evidence of his importance and to impress her even more, he convinced himself that he needed the seldom-used car, which was parked only a few hundred feet from the dock. At eight o'clock in the evening, dressed entirely in white, Peter jump-started the car and went off to join the girl of his dreams. At 2 A.M., drunk as a skunk, he reparked the car and came back on board.

Onassis was off making a tour of the principal nightclubs of Monte Carlo and didn't return until five in the morning. He might have been back a good deal sooner if that hadn't been the night when he got into an argument with a coat-check girl. As I've said, Onassis is very generous with his money, but at the same time he has a horror of being considered a man that just anyone can tap for a few extra dollars. By three o'clock, Onassis and his party were the only ones left in this particular place, and his raincoat was the only garment checked with the girl. Deciding that she'd like to go home, she marched out to Onassis' table and ostentatiously placed the coat on a chair. She then brazenly waited around for him to give her a tip. Quite to the contrary, Onassis motioned her to take back the coat and, just to annoy her and demonstrate that he was the one who decided when the place shut down and the employees could go home, he stayed until five o'clock.

Finally, however, his coat over his shoulder, Onassis strolled back along quai Grimaldi toward the *Christina*. Suddenly, in the distance, he saw a young blond girl literally beating up a sky-blue Austin with a length of pipe. He hurried over to find the girl just finishing on the windshield. Maintaining his usual calm, Onassis continued to observe this "Fury" who had now started in on the headlights, not in the least hindered by the presence of a stranger. Concluding that his entire car would be subjected to the same treatment, Onassis tried to find out why she was ruining something that didn't belong to her. Without having to be asked twice, the German girl poured out her story, without diminishing her attack on the car.

The automobile, she told him, belonged to a desperate character who'd driven her about seven miles toward Nice, stopped in the middle of nowhere and tried to rape her. "Since I resisted his attack," she said, "the rotten bastard left me on the roadside to return on foot." Her seven-mile walk had given her plenty of time to gather up a storm of resentment and anger, which she was now taking out on his car, easily recognizable there on the street.

The last window was about to go when Onassis introduced himself, informing her that the car belonged to him and that one of his men had undoubtedly been the culprit. He cordially invited her to come to lunch the next day, and in the meantime, offered to escort her home. As she lived only a few houses away, this was not necessary, but she promised to be there for her revenge as planned. Needless to say, Onassis, who'd remained calm during this conversation, was in a rage, and could hardly wait to take his fury out on us.

Between courses at lunch the following day, Peter boasted of his sexual prowess, regaling us with all the juicy details of his night spent with the beautiful girl. Onassis aptly chose this very moment to make his entrance, accompanied by the supposed object of these exploits, who pointed out her assailant immediately. Onassis proceeded to tell the whole story as it really happened, and only fired Peter when he considered him sufficiently humiliated in front of the crew. He did, however, use his powers of persuasion to convince the young girl not to press charges against the sailor, more to save himself trouble and the prospect of sordid headlines, I think, than to keep his ex-employee out of jail.

This episode was really the last straw. Onassis told us once again that he'd had enough of our dishonesty; he would no longer lend us anything, and we were henceforth required to be back on the yacht either no later than midnight or no earlier than six in the morning. For months afterward, you could see many a sailor from the *Christina* hanging around the bars in Monte Carlo, waiting for the dawn.

3 | Sir Winston

To our great surprise, Rozas, Onassis' Paris chauffeur, arrived one evening in Monte Carlo, driving the Rolls-Royce.

I must explain why we were particularly amazed to see this car so far away from its regular home. The Rolls was new in 1949, but still in perfect condition eleven years later, because of one major defect: it had never gotten more than five miles to the gallon, which seemed rather excessive, even to a millionaire like Onassis. Rozas himself didn't know why he'd been summoned and we couldn't understand why Onassis had gone to this enormous expense when he already had his other chauffeur, Jeannot, with him, as well as a number of cars: the Mercedes, a Mercury station wagon, Tina's black Ford and the famous sky-blue Austin. He even had a vehicle on the stern of the *Christina* next to the hydroplane, which he could use on those occasions when he didn't hire a limousine to meet him in foreign ports.

Before I continue, perhaps I should tell you a little bit about Rozas, who's quite an extraordinary person. After at least fifteen years of service, he belongs, like

George, Hélène and Achilles, to the old guard of servants devoted to Onassis. But Rozas has one enormous fault: he's absolutely unable to get up on time in the morning. For a number of reasons, Onassis is generally patient with him, but finally, exasperated at having to wait at least fifteen minutes every morning, he installed an enormous clock over Rozas' bed. The alarm could be controlled electrically and George was in charge of setting it off at eight o'clock every morning. But the alarm turned out to be so loud that Onassis let himself in for a whole new headache; people constantly complained because they thought the building was on fire or that someone was stuck in the elevator. Worse still, Rozas continued to be late.

It must be said in his defense, though, that very few people would be willing to drive for Onassis in Paris, since he never goes to bed before three or four in the morning. Moreover, Onassis rarely drives himself anywhere after his frightening accident of 1954. He was at the wheel of a fifteen-horsepower tractor crossing a bridge, when suddenly he was blinded by the sun; he knocked down the railing and managed to come to a stop only a few inches from the edge.

So, in spite of his one failing, Rozas is an excellent and discreet employee, and someone whom Onassis can always count upon. His arrival in Monte Carlo could only mean that Onassis was expecting a very important person.

As it turned out, the next morning Onassis got into the Rolls and headed for the airport at Nice, returning an hour later with four people: Sir Winston and Lady Churchill; his doctor, Lord Moran; and Sir Winston's bodyguard.

I must say here that among all the important people I had occasion to see while I worked for Onassis, none impressed me as much as Churchill. He was the kind of person who made you feel like standing at attention. You could even see a change in the great millionaire himself. Onassis was very different when he was with his friend, almost like a small boy, full of admiration and respect.

Churchill was elegantly dressed, sporting a navy-blue polka-dot bow tie. As he boarded the *Christina*, he walked slowly and painfully. The small crowd gathered on the dock started to applaud, and Onassis, who generally never pays the slightest attention to idle bystanders of this kind, smiled happily at them; he was undoubtedly pleased to have the arrival of his old friend appreciated in this fashion. Churchill made a slight bow to the people on the dock, then addressed the members of the crew with a smart, "Good morning, gentlemen."

To my mind Churchill had two very striking physical traits. To begin with, although his eyes were relatively small, they expressed so much strength and kindness, mixed with irony and mistrust, that it was impossible to divine his thoughts. Secondly, his hands were disproportionately small in relation to his body, and he held his proverbial cigar with unusual elegance between his thumb and middle finger. In addition, Churchill always carried his black cane with the silver knob which he held between his knees when sitting. He rarely was seen without a hat, indoors or out, the presence of women notwithstanding. When wearing a white suit, he discarded his gray felt in favor of an enormous straw

Panama, and once I even saw him sporting a naval officer's hat.

In contrast to her husband, Lady Churchill had the air of a charming and warmhearted grandmother. She usually wore simple, rather long cotton-print dresses. Because of the extreme aura of kindliness and goodwill about her, I'm tempted to compare her to Mrs. de Gaulle. They both seemed to create the same atmosphere of watchful understanding and discretion, somewhat like the benevolence of a guardian angel.

Onassis made a much greater effort to appear well dressed when his friend was aboard, and more often than not wore a jacket and tie, as well as imitating Sir Winston's neatly pleated pocket handkerchief.

The evening of their arrival, Tina appeared in a long dress, while Onassis and the other men wore dinner jackets to honor Churchill, who was similarly dressed. When Sir Winston was on the *Christina,* Onassis allowed no one to ignore this rule of etiquette.

During dinner, the only wine served was champagne. Churchill only drank Dom Perignon with his meals, although he would have a glass of straight whiskey before dinner, and ate his cheese after dinner accompanied by a half-glass of port.

These evenings with Churchill were calm and dignified, although the conversation was of necessity quite loud because the elderly statesman was somewhat deaf. Around 11:30 P.M., though, after he'd retired for the night, the atmosphere changed completely. Onassis immediately took off his shoes, undid his bow tie and discarded his jacket. If he'd been irritated by something that happened during the day, the departure of Sir

Winston at night would even bring back the usual stormy expression he'd managed to shake off earlier in order to present a serene countenance to his friend.

Onassis actually spent his free time during the day taking care of Churchill in every way. In return, the older gentleman was very grateful. They spent most of their time together playing cards, usually gin rummy. Sometimes, as an innocent amusement, Onassis had the swimming pool emptied and the bottom electrically raised to the level of the deck. He would then put two chairs in the center so that he and Churchill could be carried up and down at will. Churchill greatly enjoyed this game until one day when the floor got stuck in the down position. There was no danger in this, but Churchill didn't have sufficient strength at his age to climb out of the swimming pool himself. Onassis ordered the engineer to fix the motor at once, but fifteen minutes went by and no progress had been made.

Everyone could see that Onassis was getting more and more exasperated at this ridiculous situation, imagining the awkwardness of engineering his friend's removal from the bottom. Onassis would never have shown anger in front of Churchill, however, and made a heroic effort to keep smiling and chatting amiably.

After twenty minutes, he resummoned the engineer, Kimon, and spoke to him rapidly in Greek. "How many stripes on your hat?"

"How many—?"

"How many *stripes* on your freaking *hat?*"

"Uh—four, sir."

"You know what you can *do* with those stripes, don't you?"

"Yes, sir."

"If you don't fix this floor, you know what you can *do* with them!"

"Yes, sir."

"You can *jam* those stripes on your hat! You can *jam* them!"

Intrigued by the Greek word *skoufos* that he'd heard Onassis repeat, Churchill asked him what it meant.

"Well, it means—'hat.' "

"*Hat?*" Churchill said, frowning. "Why on earth are you telling him to put on his hat to fix the God-damn swimming pool? Tell him to use a *screwdriver!*"

With Kimon still standing at attention, Onassis was obliged to pass on the message. "Mr. Churchill suggests that you use a screwdriver." He lowered his voice. "And if *that* doesn't work, I'll personally show you what else you can do with it!"

Of course, Churchill was well aware that Onassis had insulted the engineer and wanted to make fun of his irascible friend. The worst of it for Onassis was that Churchill's sage advice really worked. A few minutes later, the floor slowly started on its way up again.

"So you see, my dear friend," Sir Winston concluded, "in politics as in everyday life, common sense is the best weapon."

Smiling maliciously, he put his arm around Onassis' shoulders and walked off the platform where he'd just spent an uncomfortable half-hour.

Churchill was extremely fond of Onassis. If ever they were walking somewhere together, the older man would take his arm, and sometimes during one of their long discussions, Churchill would rest his hand gently on his friend's, in silent communication. Once I was witness to a particularly touching scene.

We were a few miles from Gibraltar and it was just about midday; Onassis was giving Churchill his whiskey. Struck by a sudden idea, he asked Churchill if he might like to try some special caviar he'd just received from Iran. Gourmet that he was, Churchill didn't have to be asked twice. The barman, Louis, came back very solemnly carrying the small crystal container resting on a bed of ice in a silver bowl. Churchill must have been especially tired that day because he tried two or three times without success to lift the small piece of buttered toast, spread with caviar and onion, which Onassis had prepared for him. He was ready to give up altogether when he finally spilled it all over himself. At this point, Onassis got to his feet, took a small spoonful of caviar and held it toward his friend, who looked back at him with an unforgettable expression—a mixture of tenderness, friendship and pain.

At the sight of this, I was so moved that I had to leave the room with tears in my eyes.

You must realize that Churchill was already eighty-five years old then, and the natural weakness of age had been aggravated by several strokes which, according to the doctors, had definitely affected his brain. (The first of these had taken place in 1949 at Monte Carlo, a fact that didn't prevent him two years later from being elected Prime Minister for a term of four years.)

Unfortunately, Sir Winston was incontinent and obliged to change his clothes several times a day. This, in fact, caused Onassis a good deal of trouble each year when Churchill came aboard, because the couple who did the laundry didn't relish this extra work at all. The whole story finally ended with their departure, but not before they'd made a tidy profit from the awkward situation.

It started the previous year. The day before the *Christina* was to set off with the Churchills for New York, the couple let Onassis know, via the second mate, that they were not coming without a substantial raise in salary. To avoid inconvenience, Onassis doubled their pay and they stayed with the ship.

But this time, during our cruise around the Mediterranean to Spain, Italy and Greece, the couple finally decided to give notice. When Onassis found out why they were leaving (he was perfectly aware of his friend's state of health, though he never spoke about it to anyone), he went to the laundry himself in a towering rage.

"You can both go to hell!" he told them. "Nobody will miss you in the slightest! I'll wash Mr. Churchill's clothes myself, if necessary!"

In fact, I'm sure he would have, if another couple hadn't been hired right away and brought by hydroplane to Gibraltar, where the *Christina* had anchored.

The original couple, with their combined savings and severance pay, were able to set up a large cleaning establishment in Monte Carlo, which is still there today, on the Boulevard d'Italie. It later turned out that they'd also weaseled money out of Churchill, which is even more extraordinary, since he absolutely never tipped Onassis' employees on the yacht.

Churchill's way of saying thank you for the constant attention and service he received was to give everyone a personally inscribed photograph. In addition, the officers received one of his famous cigars. But this couple had the audacity to approach Sir Winston's bodyguard, who had no idea that his employer was the cause of their departure the very next day. "Tell Mr. Churchill that at the very least we would like to have an inscribed photograph," they commanded. The same night, they received their photographs, along with a certain sum of money. I could never find out exactly how much it was, nor do I know whether Churchill regarded this money as a bribe, or if he actually realized how much extra work he'd caused these people.

It was true that Churchill's presence on board cut down a great deal on everybody's free time, mainly because Onassis became extremely demanding when his friend was around; everything had to be just right. Somehow or other we were always expected to be there when the great man required something, but of course completely invisible, so as not to disturb him.

But the worst of our problems was getting on and off the ship when in port. Normally, crew and guests alike were allowed to use the same gangway, but with Churchill aboard, only the family, their guests and the officers were eligible for this privilege. The rest of us were obliged to disembark via an opening on the port side, something that eventually got me into trouble with the boss.

One night in Gibraltar, I was getting ready to go ashore after work. I knew that I had to use the side exit. That afternoon carpenters and mechanics had been busy rigging up a system of pulleys and ropes so that we could cross over the hundred feet or so that separated us from the dock. First we had to glide down a rope into a tiny boat that bobbed unsteadily in the water. Then we had to pull on another rope that would tow this frail little craft into the dock. Tired as we were at the end of a long day, and in all probability dressed for an evening out on the town, this maneuver was very inconvenient, to say the least.

I was just trying to decide how to get down without dirtying my white sweater when, as luck would have it, I found myself face to face with the boss. He must have been on his way to check on the morale of the crew, which he'd heard was low because of the gymnastics required to get ashore.

I turned away, hoping to avoid this confrontation, but it was too late; he called my name. As casually as possible, I wandered over and asked him what he wanted. Instead of answering, he stared long and hard at my sweater, walked all the way around to the back and, facing me again, quietly asked where the name had gone. He was referring to the name CHRISTINA, which had been sewn onto four beautiful white wool sweaters from London, given to me when I started work.

As it happened, in order to be able to avoid the endless questions about the private life of Onassis, I'd cut the letters off two of the sweaters, so that I could use them for going ashore. Since the whole world knew that Churchill was aboard, it was even harder to avoid being approached, especially by reporters. Although Onassis had found me out, I decided to try and play it dumb.

"What!" I said. "You mean they aren't *there* anymore?"

"I guess they must have disintegrated," he told me.

I was lucky that night, and was given a chance to explain how impossible it was to wear those sweaters ashore.

"Oh, I understand," Onassis sympathized. "You're

scared stiff everyone will take you for the owner of the *Christina* and ask you for money!"

More seriously, though, he was anxious to know what sort of things people wanted to find out, and I added that only a few days before, in Monte Carlo, a reporter from one of the large American monthly magazines had offered me five thousand dollars (almost four years' pay for a sailor) to tell him everything that happened on the *Christina.*

"What did you do?" Onassis asked, intrigued.

"I refused the offer and told him that what went on aboard ship didn't interest me."

Onassis looked at me a long time, then smiled. "Continue ashore," he said. "Have a ball, you deserve it!"

One afternoon I witnessed yet another instance of Onassis' constant desire to entertain his friend. This time it was Churchill who, by accident, invented a new game to amuse the group. He'd been eating a salad over by the railing and accidentally dropped his plate overboard. By chance, five or six dolphins were following the ship and started playing with the shiny object. Delighted, Sir Winston called Onassis' attention to this phenomenon and Onassis sent me for more plates. Having been warned what they were for, I naturally reached for the pile of ordinary white plates reserved for the help. But when Onassis saw them, he got furious and yelled: "What do you mean by bringing me these! Get my *own* plates!" I made another trip to bring up the blue-and-white Limoges service, which were worth at least twenty dollars apiece. Normally, I don't believe Onassis would've used one of his four best sets of china for this charming diversion, but I think he wanted to show the world how he treasured Churchill's regard for him. The two men must have played for a half-hour; only when the last saucer was gone did the dolphins disappear in the distance.

Along the same theme, I recall the incident of the baklava. It so happened that Churchill, in spite of his many trips to Greece, confessed one evening that he'd never tasted this national specialty. As always, when Greece was under discussion, Onassis went on at length about the excellence of this dessert. Although we were headed for Athens at the time, he couldn't wait even a few days to present his guest with a baklava, and the next day secretly sent the hydroplane off to fetch one. That night, proud as a schoolboy, he had the superb cake set before Churchill after the cheese course.

Churchill knew exactly how to acknowledge this generous gesture. One day soon after, he stayed in his cabin all day and even ordered in sandwiches for lunch. The same night, with the aid of the carpenter and Tina, who was in charge of keeping her husband out of the room, he was able to hang a completed painting on the wall of the lounge.

I must interject here that Churchill rarely had the strength to paint anymore; he found that his hands trembled and the long hours of concentration tired him too much.

When Onassis was allowed to return, he didn't see anything different right away, although he commented upon the smell of fresh paint. Sir Winston, feigning astonishment, said he didn't notice anything special. When Onassis finally caught sight of the painting, however, he admired it very enthusiastically and thanked his friend with particular warmth, knowing how great an effort it must have been.

I've been on many a cruise with Onassis when a variety of different guests were aboard—Tito, Liz Taylor, Jacqueline Kennedy—but I never saw him as happy as when he was with Churchill. He was in a good mood every day, which was quite unusual for him. What's more, Tina and Lady Churchill got along so well and the group had such a good time together that no one could possibly imagine the Onassises would one day be divorced.

After the three-week cruise was over, Sir Winston and Lady Churchill left for London. It was the last week in July. Tina and the children settled once again into the Château de la Croé and Onassis went back to work, which for him meant traveling all over the world. He usually spent no more than five or six days a month on the Riviera with his family.

4 | A Fabulous Success Story

Onassis is one of those people who can never really seem to totally forget his work, even during his few weeks of summer vacation. For instance, during the hours when he was not with Sir Winston, he shut himself up in his office aboard ship to go over the numerous cables that were transmitted over the *Christina*'s radio at all times of the night or day. What's more, whenever he was ashore, he made a beeline for a restaurant or a hotel to telephone his replies. It's true that every cabin on the *Christina* has a phone, but since in most ports it's impossible to attach the vessel to telephone wires, they're largely useless except in Monte Carlo and Skorpios, and after Onassis' fight with Prince Rainier, the *Christina* has never returned to Monte Carlo.

On Skorpios, though, Onassis has a special switchboard where the operators relieve each other every eight hours so he can conduct his business in countries around the world; often he has to receive or make phone calls in the middle of the night, depending on the time zone of the place in question. (After their marriage Jackie soon found that she didn't have a quiet moment when she was with her husband in New York, the telephone rang so often, no matter what time it was.)

It's only fair to say that Onassis has an abundant source of energy and needs very little sleep to keep going. When he doesn't have a dinner engagement, he usually eats in a restaurant, comes home well before midnight and stays up working until three in the morning. He then goes to bed at four and is up again by eight. After lunch, he takes an hour's nap. He spends his days working in his office, but he's forced to spend evenings on the phone, usually to New York, Paris, London, Athens and South America, where his main offices are. It's no wonder that Jackie asked her husband to find a solution to the problem, especially since, in addition to the noise of the phone, Onassis is in the habit of wandering all around the house, speaking to himself in monologues. I discovered the truth of this "legend" one night in Monte Carlo soon after one of our cruises with the Churchills.

Around eleven o'clock I was on deck smoking a final cigarette before going to bed. All of a sudden Onassis appeared on the main deck below, walking with his hands behind his back, talking, then stopping from time to time before going on again. I could hear his voice only intermittently because of the gusts of wind that evening, but I definitely thought he was with someone I simply couldn't see; the enormous smokestack blocked my view. But when he finally reached the bow, there was no longer any doubt: he was speaking to himself in Greek.

That night I made a great discovery, perhaps even learned a secret of this man's success. I saw Onassis spend two solid hours asking himself out loud all the questions that he might have to answer before going to a particular meeting or appointment. He answered everything as if he had an actual audience. Sometimes he would take a few seconds to think over a reply, other times he would answer very rapidly, maybe pretending to get angry. He even practiced saying nothing, merely nodding his head in reply to an imaginary question. This is how I found out that Onassis rehearses his lines just like an actor, and at the same time tries to anticipate and outguess his opponents.

Naturally, this habit doesn't bother anyone when Onassis is on the boat or when he walks along empty streets as he sometimes does. It's no wonder, though, that Jackie made him keep his old apartment in the Pierre Hotel in New York; consider for a moment what it would be like having him go through this routine, in the tradition of Demosthenes, while they lived together in a New York apartment.

I once went to the Pierre to find out Onassis' average monthly telephone bill. I was told that it was difficult to ascertain, since he uses four private lines in addition to the hotel phone, but from what I was able to gather, he must pay no less than $8,000 a month; around $100,-000 a year.

This must seem like rather a lot, but of course it's only a drop in the bucket compared to what he takes in every year from all his different companies, something in the neighborhood of $70,000,000. It's impossible, naturally, to assess Onassis' annual income. One of his directors once told him that to compute an exact figure would take all his secretaries and accountants at least two years, working full-time.

To show how Onassis managed to arrive at this position of power and wealth, we have to go back a half-century. I would like to start by saying that most of what has already been written on this subject is a pack of lies. What I've done is to find a wide variety of people who knew Onassis at the beginning of his career; since most of them live in different countries and knew Onassis at different times, I'm ready to vouch for the truthfulness of their statements.

Aristotle Onassis was born in 1906 in Smyrna, Turkey. His father Socrates is said to have been a tobacco trader there in the heart of Turkey; but in fact, that was only much later, in Greece, after Ari had made his way to Argentina. Originally, Socrates ran an operation for sponge diving with a dozen or so boats and forty to fifty skindivers, who worked along the east coast of the Aegean Sea. Nor was the family badly off at that time. Ari and his three sisters went to excellent schools and by the time he was sixteen, he spoke fluent Spanish, English, Turkish and Greek.

In talking with Kostas Koutchouvelis, who was then one of Onassis' playmates, I found out that at a very early age Ari had a talent for business. Kostas' mother, in fact, was instrumental in starting the young boy on his first business venture.

One day when Ari was only fifteen, he asked Kostas and his brother George if their mother couldn't lend him the money to buy a four-thousand-ton vessel that he'd seen for sale. Mrs. Koutchouvelis already had a small fleet of ships that sailed between Turkey, Greece and Argentina, and the brothers spoke so highly of their friend that she not only lent Ari the money, but hired him as her secretary.

Ari immediately chartered his ship to an African company and after four months he'd already earned back enough money to pay off his debt to Mrs. Koutchouvelis. Much later in life, George Koutchouvelis became admiral of the Onassis fleet; Kostas became the tutor of Onassis' son Alexandre.

In 1922, the Turks decided to reclaim all the land they had lost to the Greeks during World War I, and the Onassis family was badly hit. Several of them were executed and others died in a church that was set on fire. Mrs. Onassis and her three daughters managed to escape the carnage, but Ari and his father were thrown in prison, to be executed three days later. By some miracle, the vice-consul of Smyrna intervened on their behalf and father and son were able to leave Turkey for Piraeus.

Another friend, George Sevdayan, picked up the story from here:

"It was 1922, around May or June, and I remember distinctly the day that I first saw Aristotle. I was selling cigarettes in the street and I saw a very handsome young boy peddling newspapers. Though not very tall, he had particularly penetrating eyes. For several days we ran into each other without speaking, but one thing struck me right away. In spite of his shabby clothes, he was totally different from the other poor kids in the streets of Piraeus. He already had an outstanding personality. From the day we finally got to talking with one another, we became fast friends."

George insisted that Ari was even then on his way to becoming a millionaire. He never kept any money on him. Instead, he used his profits from selling newspapers to buy anything he thought he could make money on—from tobacco and wrist watches to statuettes and exotic animals—mostly from sailors returning from long voyages. Once, he even had a monkey for sale.

After eight months in Piraeus, Ari had managed to

save a certain sum of money and told George that he was thinking of emigrating. A few days later the future millionaire was on his way to Argentina. George went on to tell me about a coincidence that occurred many years later as he was eating in a restaurant in Paris. The owner happened to start chatting with him and confided that one day Onassis had confessed how much he would enjoy seeing his old friend George from Piraeus. George knew right away that Onassis must have been talking about him and accordingly went home and wrote Onassis a long letter saying that he would be happy to meet again after all these years and that in addition he would welcome some advice on investing a certain sum of money.

Unfortunately, this was in the winter of 1958, and Onassis was receiving more than two hundred letters a day from Greek refugees begging for help. That's why, to his great surprise, George got an answer a few days later from a secretary stating that Mr. Onassis already had too many refugees to take care of. Hurt and annoyed at this response, George never wrote again.

In reading this book, I think Onassis will be happy to know that he can now find this old friend.

After stopping in Genoa, Onassis took a freighter to Argentina. He had a small amount of money, the address of an uncle living in Buenos Aires, and a passport, which had been "corrected" so that he would be over twenty-one, the necessary age to immigrate. (The date 1906 had been changed to 1900.) On the trip, he acquired one more thing. He became friendly with a Frenchman and when he landed two months later, he was fluent in French, his fifth language.

His uncle eventually got him a job with the telephone company. A couple of months later, he worked as a night switchboard operator. It was here that he learned to get along with a minimum of sleep. He would quit work at 6 A.M. and go upstairs to bed in a hotel, where he had a small room. But after no more than three hours, he would be back in town again, looking for things to buy and sell, just as he had in Piraeus. He even took to repairing pleasure boats to get a little extra cash. In the meantime, he lived on practically nothing, eating tomatoes, bread and (three times a week) a good piece of meat. He didn't drink or smoke, although tobacco provided the first rung on the ladder to success and fortune.

One day he happened to run into a friend on the street who complained about the dry, strawlike tobacco he was forced to smoke in Argentina. He claimed that the Turks and the Greeks were very lucky to have such good tobacco. Onassis realized an opportunity: he would import tobacco from home. He was able to get his own ship back because the war between Greece and Turkey was over (1923) and he wrote his father, who was enthusiastic about this brilliant idea, to get in touch with Mrs. Koutchouvelis, who again advanced the necessary money.

In one year, Onassis had a $100,000 business, and in two years the ratio of imported tobacco had jumped from 5 to 35 percent. A short time later he became the acting Greek consul in Buenos Aires.

During the next nine years, the business continued to grow. As a diplomat he met everyone, Greeks and Argentines alike, who wanted to go to Piraeus and needed a job. This gave him the opportunity of hiring them as crew for a couple of small ships. The ships had cost him little for they were in bad condition. He didn't have to pay these men as much as regular sailors who, it seems, wouldn't work for him anyway since they considered his ships too dangerous. It was also rumored that Onassis could not get any insurance company in Buenos Aires to risk covering him. By 1927, Onassis was importing wool, grain and whale oil, as well as tobacco.

In 1931, he was able to buy six freighters from Canada for $120,000, and he put them to work as tramp, or "vagabond," steamers on noncommercial routes.

By 1933, Onassis was a millionaire several times over and he resigned as consul. In 1938, he had his first oil transport ship built and named it the *Ariston*. The outbreak of the war, which was disastrous for most shipping-line owners the world over, enabled Onassis to multiply his fortune by ten: the Germans didn't attack ships flying the Argentine colors.

At the end of the war, a new—if somewhat less than legal—opportunity presented itself. Toward the end of 1946, the United States Government decided to sell certain surplus vessels. Some of these ships, which were nicknamed "Liberty" and "Victory" ships, were dry-cargo vessels that had been mass-produced to meet emergency war needs. The Liberty ships could carry loads of 10,000 tons, the Victory ships 11,000. Also for sale were surplus T-2 tankers.

The only condition the U.S. Government placed on their sale was that they be bought by Americans. This detail didn't stop Onassis. Immediately, he formed six American companies to buy twenty-three ships for him.

In October, 1953, the government discovered the truth and sued. The case was settled in 1955, and the U.S. eventually won $7,000,000 in damages. Onassis also agreed to reorganize his American companies so that they were under effective U.S. control. But during the time he'd owned the vessels, shipping cargoes of oil, iron and machinery, he'd earned many times the amount he eventually had to pay in damages.

Another important date in Onassis' rise to fortune was 1952, when he made a trip to the Near East.

He decided to name one of his largest oil transports after Ibn Saud, the king of Saudia Arabia, and had that nation's symbol—a sword—painted under the name. Before leaving, he filled the boat with enough presents to stock an entire department store, some destined for the king himself, others for his subjects.

On landing at the port, Al Calif, Onassis graciously distributed part of his cargo to the crowd that greeted him before being taken to the Riad palace, where he formally offered the monarch many precious stones, bracelets and silver. The least expensive but most precious gift was a magnificent pair of canaries. Onassis had long been in the habit of traveling with his favorite canary, Caruso, and from that moment on, Ibn Saud imitated the millionaire.

In fact, a rather touching story grew out of their first meeting. Some years later, Ibn Saud and his retinue left Paris for Switzerland in two planes, one of which crashed with no survivors. A few days later the king telephoned Onassis to say that the canaries had been with him in the first plane and were safe and sound.

But to get back to this original meeting, the two men signed a contract in which Olympic Maritime was given the right to transport 10 percent of Saudia Arabia's oil throughout the world. The festival that followed this momentous event was fantastic. The king had an elaborate parade in Onassis' honor before returning to the palace for an evening of exotic entertainment; but the most memorable part of the whole evening was the dinner.

The main course consisted of "stuffed camel," which was prepared in the following manner. First, a camel was slit open down the center, the entrails removed and the cavity cleaned. Next, the camel was stuffed with a skinned deer, which had been treated in the same way. Then the deer was stuffed with a lamb, and so on, until there was just enough room for a dove. Finally, the camel's stomach was sewn up and the whole thing was roasted on a spit for twelve hours, while constantly turned and basted with special oils flavored with the exotic spices of the country.

Following this extraordinary dinner, Onassis left by plane, taking with him the precious contract and two solid gold swords, presents from the king, that now adorn the walls of his office on the *Christina.*

A significant aspect of Onassis' genius for business is his ability to anticipate events. When Nasser decided to take over the Suez Canal, for example, everyone else's ships were stranded in Iran, except Onassis'; each of his vessels continued to make four thousand dollars a day.

One of his major characteristics in business is not to give an inch to a competitor, whoever he may be. One day, for instance, Stavros Niarchos came to see him on the *Christina* and mentioned that he was interested in buying a 10,000-ton ship, the *Pénépoli,* which was for sale at a very good price in Marseilles. Onassis was also aware of this deal but until that point had been in no hurry, since he thought he was the only one interested in the ship. On hearing this, however, he asked to be excused for a moment and left Niarchos sipping whiskey, while he radioed ashore that he wanted to buy the *Pénépoli* immediately.

When he returned, Niarchos picked up the conversation and asked him what he thought about the deal. Onassis admitted that he thought it excellent, but that unfortunately the boat was already sold.

"And to whom?" Niarchos asked, very surprised.

"Why, to me, of course," he said, with a smile.

In 1956, Onassis founded Olympic Airways. At that time, Greece had three small airlines operated by the government, with a total of no more than five hundred employees. Onassis negotiated for a fifty-year contract, combining the three carriers into one—Olympic Airways. A few months after he took control, around Easter, Onassis decided to honor the old Greek custom of sending each of his employees a live sheep. In order to be practical, he sent each recipient the gift at home. One young errand boy who found a lamb in front of his sixth-floor apartment decided to quit his job, offered to take care of his colleagues' sheep as well and started a growing business. Each day he took his flock out behind the Acropolis and soon had enough capital either to buy the lambs outright or pay interest on a loan to cover the price.

Of course, Onassis was bound to hear about this eventually. He called the young man into his office, congratulated him warmly on his cleverness and rewarded him with a piece of land to pasture his sheep a mile or two outside of Athens.

Onassis rapidly made Olympic Airways one of the most successful carriers in the world. But perhaps more importantly, he initiated a special airline service for the poor. He instructed his staff that all sick children, especially polio victims, who needed hospitalization or a doctor, would be transported to Athens free; if there was no space on a scheduled flight, a special taxi-plane would be made available. The children were usually taken to Saint Sophy Hospital, which specialized in children's diseases.

Before he took over Olympic Airways, Onassis had bought 520,000 shares of a company named Société des Bains de Mer, in Monte Carlo, which turned out to be not only one of his worst investments but the catalyst for his rupture with Prince Rainier, as I mentioned earlier. Contrary to what has been written on the subject, the difference that ended their many years of friendly relations started with a favor that Onassis rendered to his good friend Embiricos.

The stock that Onassis bought in 1952 gave him complete control of the casino, but involved so much work that by 1959 he decided to hire someone to take over this responsibility. Embiricos suggested that one of his cousins who had lost all his money in the stock market in New York needed a job and would be an excellent choice. Onassis met with the prospect, Marakis Embiricos, and after some reflection, hired him for the job.

Marakis undoubtedly had many talents, but he simply couldn't make a success of the casino. First, he spent a great deal of money redesigning the gardens, redoing the bowling alley and the Café de Paris, without increasing the profits at all. As a result, the stock began a steady decline.

Finally, by 1966, Prince Rainier was tired of seeing the operation progressively deteriorate in the hands of all these Greeks. The prince asked Onassis to sell his stock.

As you can imagine, Onassis is not the kind of man who would want to stick around after somebody has shown him the door. Moreover, he was insulted that the prince thought he was not taking care of Monte Carlo as he had promised. Accordingly, Onassis offered to sell for $40,000,000. Prince Rainier could take it or leave it.

Rainier didn't agree. He suggested $8,000,000 and threatened to arrange that Onassis would no longer be the major stockholder if he refused this offer. Onassis had no choice but to accept.

Most people thought that Onassis' investment in Monte Carlo earned him a great deal of money, but that is completely untrue. Although he did manage to double his investment, the same amount invested at a mere 5 percent over fourteen years would have netted him the same profit. Needless to say, Onassis was not one who made his fortune by investing his money at such a low rate of return. The only good thing to come of this risk, which he took out of friendship for Maris Embiricos, was that he kept the old winter sports building, which still houses the Monte Carlo offices of Olympic Maritime.

I would like to conclude this chapter with a story

that in a way goes against all of Onassis' principles of good business. One day in August, 1960, he was expected to arrive at Glyfada in the afternoon. I was one of the individuals scheduled to meet him on shore with the Chris-Craft and transport him to the *Christina*, which had been at anchor in the bay for over two weeks. The usual crowd had gathered at the port and some policemen were on hand to preserve order. Onassis was quite late in arriving, and without wasting any more time he went straight from the car to the vessel, not stopping to speak to anyone. The engines were already running and the Chris-Craft was just about to cast off when a young boy broke through the police lines and plunged fully clothed into the water, crying: "Mr. Onassis, I absolutely have to talk to you! I'm from a very poor family and my name is Zacherias; I have lots of brothers and sisters and I simply *must* speak to you!"

Onassis slowed the boat and we helped the boy climb aboard, to be taken out to the *Christina* a mile away.

It seemed that George Zacherias had one ambition: to save his family from destitution by raising chickens. He explained that he would like Onassis to become his partner; he already had the land and a couple of dozen chickens.

"If you will invest two thousand dollars in this venture," he said, "we can buy another eight hundred chicks and the necessary equipment to raise them properly." He assured Onassis, who listened gravely, that the sale of the eggs and the chicks would put them in big business. Onassis asked for forty-eight hours to consider the proposition, and George was taken ashore again. This was when I heard the whole story of the twenty-minute interview.

After checking that George was telling the truth and was really the honest young fellow he appeared to be, Onassis gave him the money, saying as he did so, "If I'm ever in need of anything in life, I'll always know that I can count on at least one egg a day!"

Unfortunately, two years later, a disease killed all the chickens and George was due to go off to military service. When he returned, he was anxious to start all over again, but Onassis told him it was not profitable enough. Instead, he got him a job working for Princess Lee Radziwill.

It may seem surprising that Onassis, who juggles enormous sums of money every day, would be willing to waste his time with a poor boy's ambition to raise chickens. In reality, Onassis is always ready to listen to those who need him, especially the young. He has never forgotten that his own start in life was also made possible by adults who were willing to trust him.

5 | Fun and Games

Two things have always impressed me about Onassis: his ability to get along with all kinds of people and the simplicity of his taste in amusements.

He's the complete opposite of all those socialites and celebrities who consider it essential to make appearances in the most fashionable places accompanied by the usual retinue of dilettantes and hangers-on. I know that one day Jackie asked him why he made it such a point to avoid almost every party and social event.

Onassis considered the question carefully. "I simply don't have the time," he told her quietly. "I don't have time for Punch and Judy shows."

But after his divorce from Tina, and especially during his years with Maria Callas, things were somewhat different for a while. Although he continued to avoid gala social functions, he didn't shy away from having a good time. And, without falling into excess, he seemed to enjoy letting himself go.

Listening to popular music has always been one of his favorite pastimes, especially the Bouzouki and the Argentine tango, but he simply abhors classical music.

For example, when Maria used to accompany herself on the piano while practicing in the lounge of the *Christina,* he'd usually escape to the tranquillity of his office.

Onassis' favorite nightclub is Zampétas, on Glyfada, where he can invite all his old friends and—if the spirit moves him—break as many plates as he likes. He feels uninhibited and very much at home there where he always adds a rather unique personal touch when dancing the *sirtaki.* After choosing a male partner from his own group or somebody from the crowd, Onassis and the other man grab corners of a table napkin. The napkin supports the person who is dancing on one foot or making a fast turn. In a single fast motion, Onassis then shoves his free hand into his pocket, whips out a bill from the famous roll he always has with him, licks it, and sticks it on the forehead of one of the musicians. Since he might do this trick many times in one evening, the night rarely ends before he's spent several thousand dollars.

Onassis isn't a snob. Aside from the necessary social obligations his money and standing require of him, he generally prefers to amuse himself with relatively simple people rather than the international Jet Set. It's not at all unusual to see him spend evenings with one of his own employees or a sailor from a ship anchored next to the *Christina.*

One night in September, 1959, for instance, he happened to go into a nightclub in Monte Carlo opposite the police station, the Gypsy, where he saw Nicolas Ecaterinis, first mate of Embiricos' yacht, the *Doudouna.*

To understate the case, Nicolas wasn't exactly included among Onassis' favorite people. Tina once heard this handsome young man sing aboard Embiricos' yacht and, thinking how pleasant it would be to enjoy the same thing on the *Christina* while she took a swim, she invited him back with her. Onassis had the misfortune to arrive right in the middle of this poolside serenade. Innocent though it was, he blew his stack—ostensibly because she was amusing herself by making other people's crew members work overtime. Actually, Embiricos had warned Onassis to keep his wife and his friend's wives away from this dangerously attractive first mate, who was reputed to be the greatest Don Juan on the Riviera.

Anyway, on this particular evening in the Gypsy, Onassis had already had plenty to drink, so without hesitation he walked up to Nicolas' table, spoiling for a confrontation.

"Since you're with such a beautiful girl, how about fixing me up, too?"

Nicolas played it cool, as usual. "No problem. But with all your dough, you'd think you'd be able to find one on your own."

"Is that a fact?" Onassis sat down. "You think it's money that turns them on? I'll tell you something. It's not money, it's a pretty face like yours. That's the secret. Pure animal magnetism."

"I'm not so sure about that. You game for a little experiment?"

"Completely at your disposal," Onassis said.

Nicolas walked confidently to a nearby table, where two very attractive young girls were sitting by themselves. Onassis followed.

"Excuse me, ladies, but my friend Mr. Onassis would

like to meet you and buy you a bottle of champagne."

Blushing with obvious delight, they immediately asked Onassis to join them, peppering him with all sorts of adoring comments in Italian and French.

"You see," Nicolas told him in Greek, "money is just as persuasive as beauty!"

As it turned out, Onassis decided that he would much rather spend the rest of the evening with the first mate than in the company of the two girls. A few drinks later, he went back to Nicolas' table.

"Hey, Romeo, how about a Greek song? Come on, come on, I've heard you're a great singer!"

"I'll sing only on the condition that you dance."

Feeling absolutely no pain at that point, Onassis grabbed a loaded tray from one of the waiters and held it in his palm. "God damn it, I've done a lot of asinine things in my life—even waiting on tables to earn my *living!*—but I've never been reduced to dancing in public!"

"Fair enough! I never sing except for my own pleasure! If you don't have the guts to dance, I don't have the guts to sing! That's final!"

Eventually, after a convoluted conversation proving that neither of them was thinking very clearly, they came to a momentous decision. Agreeing that if they were to make a public spectacle of themselves, they might just as well go all the way, they persuaded the orchestra to follow them outside. There, on the sidewalk in front of the Gypsy, a wild new group called Beauty and the Billionaire gave their first open concert —to an absolutely riotous reception.

In a very short time an enormous and vocal crowd gathered and the police came to disperse them. But when they saw the leader of the group, they decided not to interfere. Needless to say, the next day everyone in Monaco was talking about Onassis' famous exhibition.

It goes without saying that Onassis has a good deal of difficulty in places where everyone knows him by sight; but he constantly invents new tricks to preserve his incognito. One of his favorite ploys is to rent a little pickup truck, don a hat and remove his glasses so he can go virtually anywhere without being importuned by writers and photographers. Usually he enjoys getting together with Embiricos on the *Doudouna,* where they spend very quiet evenings chatting amiably. In fact, incidents like the Gypsy evening are rare, as are those when the millionaire takes a plane to Greece (usually because he's had a fight with the woman of his life) and goes to Zampétas to vent his anger by breaking plates.

It must seem that Onassis spends a great deal of money this way, but as a rule he pays careful attention to where it goes. He never signs a check and never pays bills with cash. He expects everyone from whatever country to send the bills to his business offices, Olympic Maritime or Olympic Airways. All checks and bills are paid once a month.

Another example of his stringent care of his money is the apartment in Paris. George and Hélène are allowed ten francs per day per person for food and necessities. Every month George has to account for all the daily expenses and all the guests who've passed through. One month during 1970, George presented unusually great expenditures for food. Since Onassis hadn't been in Paris a single day that month, George was immediately asked to account for the discrepancy. It happened that Alexandre, Onassis' son, had invited a great many friends to stay over.

Another time, Onassis asked a number of friends to join him at the Pirate nightclub in Cap Martin, and as was customary there, the guests amused themselves by breaking a few dozen plates and quite a number of glasses. When the bill came in (I don't know the exact sum but it might have been as high as five thousand dollars), the director of Olympic Maritime in Monte Carlo showed it to Onassis and they both agreed it was much too high for the evening in question. Onassis refused to pay what they were asking and never went back again. In revenge, the owners of the Pirate took down the photograph of Onassis and the Greek flag and substituted Frank Sinatra and the American flag.

Obviously, these economies do not negate the plain fact that Onassis lives just as well as he pleases. He'll send his chauffeur all the way to Italy to buy a particular kind of sausage he likes to eat with his lentils or use his hydroplane as a housewife uses a supermarket cart. I remember one occasion, when the *Christina* was anchored off Glyfada, the barman notified him early in the day that they were out of his favorite ouzo.

"Don't worry," Onassis told him. "There's plenty of time to go ashore for more. *Plenty* of time."

A few hours later, totally unannounced as usual, he decided to set out to sea. By evening he was ready for his glass of ouzo, which Louis gave him by draining the last drops from several bottles. When he asked for a second, Louis had to repeat that no more was on board.

"What is this, a *concentration camp!*" he exploded.

"Send the hydroplane back right now! Buy a dozen bottles!"

I suppose it's typical of a millionaire to economize on trifling expenses and spend fortunes to indulge his particular tastes or fancies. But still.

One of Onassis' most treasured possessions is the island of Skorpios, which he finally managed to buy in 1962. Skorpios is situated in the Ionian Sea, a half-hour by helicopter from Corfu. Four islands lie opposite: Lefkas (the largest), Skorpidi, Sparti and Madura. In 1965, Onassis also bought Sparti. Although much smaller than Skorpios (which cost him $100,000), he paid $150,000 for this island, which he turned into a hunting preserve with game imported from Yugoslavia.

Naturally, he also wanted to buy Skorpidi, which belongs to Mr. Livanos, the nephew of the former minister Kanelopoulos, but in seven years of negotiations, the two men were never able to agree on a price. Onassis knew he couldn't buy Madura, since it belongs to the family of the poet Valaoritis, who want to keep the island and the single house there as a museum and shrine to the famous writer. Lefkas will certainly never be for sale because it belongs to the Greek government and has a small airport where flights from Corfu and Athens come in. The charming little port of Nidri can be seen from Skorpios and it's the site of the only restaurant on the island, owned and run by Nikos Kominates.

Since he still has an Argentine passport, Onassis had great difficulty buying his two Greek islands. To persuade the government that it would be worthwhile, he originally promised to develop tourism by turning

Skorpios into another Monte Carlo for millionaires. He got the idea in 1960 when he was asking permission to open two casinos, in Athens and Corfu. After several months of study, the government gave the necessary permission on the condition that Onassis fly a Greek flag on part of his fleet, which then sailed under the Liberian flag. He refused, calculating the taxes he would have to pay on those ships would exceed any profit he made on the casinos. A few months later, a German nobleman (who was a naturalized Greek) obtained the concession, with a clause in the contract stipulating that no one could open a casino within a thirty-mile radius of Athens.

For a long time, Onassis knew that the island of Skorpios was for sale, but he pretended not to be interested in buying it, fearing the price would skyrocket. Eventually, he decided to purchase it at a fixed price. Certainly what he paid was a good deal less than the sum he eventually spent transforming this scorpion-infested mass of prickly undergrowth into the paradise it is today.

First of all, for a period of several days, airplanes circled over the entire island, spraying thousands of gallons of chemicals to kill the dangerous snakes and insects. Then workmen took over for several months to dynamite areas where roads could be built with cement and gravel brought over from the mainland. Next came dozens of ships loaded with rich soil from Corfu, so rare trees imported from America could be planted. Onassis even started to install an electric power station, until one day he changed his mind. He had gradually fallen in love with his island and didn't want to make it another Las Vegas. Instead, he did everything in his power to preserve the peace and tranquillity of the spot, completely abandoning the idea of developing tourism. As a result, he didn't become very popular with the natives of the surrounding islands, who expected the arrival of the famous millionaire to change their fortunes.

Approximately one hundred people work for Onassis on the island, but they all live on Lefkas, with the exception of six or seven who are under the direction of Achilles, the former carpenter of the *Christina.*

Prices on these Ionian Islands are relatively high: a Fiat 600 costs about $2,300; a bottle of whiskey, $10; a pack of American cigarettes, $1. So it's no wonder that these people, who earn between $2 and $4 a day according to Greek government wages, were terribly disappointed to suddenly find out there would be no luxury hotels on their island, no Club Méditerranée, no new roads. Instead, Skorpios, which is now considered the most beautiful island in Greece, rises majestically out of the sea to constantly remind them of their disappointment.

The island has a marvelous harbor where the *Christina* anchors, and another smaller port that was dredged especially for visiting ships. Of the several houses, one is built in a Greek style and has now been given to Jackie. A charming ancient building was totally renovated and redecorated for guests. The main house is Onassis' domain and not far away is a smaller house for the servants. There's a lovely Greek Orthodox chapel, where Onassis married Jackie in 1968. And finally, a farm devoted to raising domestic animals: pigs, goats, sheep, geese, chickens and—most impressive of all—some splendid Arabian horses. In addition,

2. Jacqueline and Aristotle Onassis at Barajas Airport near Madrid, en route to Paris, 1971.

3. The *Christina,* world's largest yacht, lies at anchor in the Hudson River, New York.

Aboard the *Christina:*

4. TOP LEFT: Mosaic dance floor on main deck may be lowered electrically to become swimming pool.

5. TOP RIGHT: Portion of lounge in forward section of main cabin. (Covers on furniture and floor are removed when yacht is in use.)

6. BOTTOM LEFT: Section of main dining room, designed for seating capacity of twenty-two.

7. BOTTOM RIGHT: Bar and stools decorated with whales' teeth.

8. LEFT: Prince Rainier (in swim trunks), Princess Grace and their daughter Caroline (in front of Onassis) at Glyfada, Greece, 1961.

9. TOP: Sir Winston Churchill with Onassis in New York, following cruise in 1961.

10. Tina Onassis dancing with Duke of Windsor at party given by Elsa Maxwell, New York, 1960.

11. Elizabeth Taylor and Onassis at Lido nightclub, Paris, 1964.

12. Maria Callas and Onassis at La Scala Opera in Milan, following 1959 cruise.

13. LEFT: Miss Callas and Onassis aboard the *Christina* during 1967 cruise in Bahamas.

14. TOP: Skorpios, Onassis' privately owned island in the Ionian Sea, south of Corfu.

15. Jacqueline and Aristotle Onassis on café terrace in Villefranche-sur-Mer, France, 1969.

16. The couple in a happy moment at sidewalk café in Capri, 1969.

17. Harassed by photographers, an unhappy Jacqueline Onassis leaves Cinema Rendezvous in New York, 1969.

18. Mr. and Mrs. Onassis at private party in the new El Morocco, New York, 1971.

there's a park with deer and some ponies that belong to Caroline and John-John.

But there are two serious drawbacks to the island: a constant danger of fire because of an inordinate amount of undergrowth, and no natural water supply. Every day, twenty-five thousand gallons of water are brought over by ship and deposited in enormous cement cisterns, a service which alone must cost Onassis a fortune every year.

A certain architect from Athens who has worked for Onassis told me that all the buildings presently on the island are only temporary. Onassis has promised to build Jackie a palace before 1975, which is to be a copy of the palace in Knossos belonging to Minos, legendary king of Crete. I must say that in view of Onassis' lack of interest in houses of any kind, I'd be very much surprised if this project was ever completed; unless, of course, it's the express wish of Jackie. For the most part, the houses on Skorpios are very simply furnished, with wicker chairs, Spanish tables and good solid country furniture. Nothing particularly expensive.

When he's on the island, Onassis leads a very quiet life, sailing, fishing and taking long walks, most often at night. This last habit almost cost him his life back in November, 1967, when he was alone on the island with the servants. Maria had stayed in Paris, angry because he'd once again dashed her hopes for marriage.

Although it was raining hard, Onassis was undaunted and set out on a stroll of the island. He only got a few hundred yards from the house when he was temporarily blinded by the rain and fell into a hole about ten feet deep. The hole began filling with water and, what's worse, the sides started to cave in as he tried to escape.

No one heard his cries for help. But thanks to his flashlight and the faithful Achilles, who two hours later went out in search of his master, he escaped with nothing worse than a bad cold.

Since 1968, Onassis and Jackie have spent much of their free time on the island, talking, watching films or playing cards, preferring to stay at home for dinner. Occasionally they dine at the simple little restaurant run by Nikos, which he's grandly baptized "Maxim's." Sometimes too, they leave in the hydroplane for a night out in Glyfada or Athens. Onassis also delights in spending a great deal of time with John-John and Caroline, perhaps because his own children don't really enjoy coming to their father's island.

Onassis' children are as different from each other as night and day; since the divorce of their parents in 1960, they're now separated from each other eleven months of the year. I know very little about Christina. As a seven-year-old, she only differed from other girls of her age in being quite independent, with few friends. Her brother Alexandre interpreted this as snobbery, but I think she was simply a young girl who didn't easily become attached to people. I know Alexandre much better. He's outgoing, simple and a lot of fun. Underneath his calm exterior, he's very much like his father, with exceptional strength of character.

The first time I met the Onassis children, Christina was just a little girl who enjoyed playing with dolls, but Alexandre already had more active amusements which, indirectly, were the cause of my being in extraordinarily good shape that summer. From an early age the boy had an absolute passion for cars. He spoke of nothing but cars and motors day and night until finally Onassis gave him a small electric vehicle that would go about fifteen or twenty miles an hour. Since Alexandre was too young to be left alone in Monte Carlo, it was our job (or more precisely mine, because I was the youngest crew member on the *Christina*) to watch the young boy wherever he went with his new toy.

As you can imagine, it wasn't a relaxing job. Once behind the wheel, Alexandre floored the accelerator and was off for a stint of two or three hours, while I ran breathlessly behind. I think it was around that time in my life that I began to appreciate the calm and quiet of rainy days. I finally compromised by renting a motorbike from a fellow who worked in a bar next to Olympic Maritime.

Alexandre was very friendly with all the sailors at that time. He adored Louis, the barman. They would often build remote-controlled boats and airplanes together.

Christina was much more reserved and we rarely saw her. I do remember that she was very vain and would change her clothes three or four times a day. She also hated Greek cooking (as she still does), which used to annoy her father, whose pleasure it was to wear a tablecloth as an apron and cook a Greek or Turkish specialty. In fact, Onassis is so fond of this hobby that he's had a sort of tiny "test kitchen" installed in Paris to use whenever the inclination hits him.

I also remember that at a very early age Christina enjoyed reporting to her father everything that went on aboard the yacht, something which enraged her brother, who had a horror of telling tales.

Even from the age of twelve, Alexandre knew how to

drive, but because he was too short at the time, he had difficulty reaching the pedals. Inevitably, he was bound to have an accident.

Without telling anyone, Alexandre decided to borrow the Ford that Jeannot the chauffeur normally used. The first Onassis heard of it was from a policeman who telephoned to inform him that his son had knocked down a young woman in the street. Though she'd only suffered minor injuries, Onassis had to pay her $23,000 to hush up the affair.

It's only fair to say that Onassis was partly responsible for encouraging this dangerous passion in his son. For his fourteenth birthday, Onassis gave him an R6, somewhat later a Ford Anglia and after that a Floride, even though everyone knew the boy didn't have his driver's license at the time. Alexandre had to wait for the license until his sixteenth birthday when he took a special trip to the United States. He passed the test with flying colors and upon his return was presented with a red Ferrari. This racing car, which of course he drove like a madman, was the indirect cause of a number of incidents and accidents.

My friend Nicolas, who was great friends with Alexandre, told me a good deal about these adventures. It seems that Alexandre preferred to drive at night when both his father and tutor were asleep. He'd sneak out the service entrance to meet Nicolas and the two of them would set off for a nocturnal spin.

"I remember one time," Nicolas told me, "we were on the Champs Élysées going at least a hundred miles per hour, when suddenly we passed two policemen who were making an inspection tour on their bicycles. All innocence, Alexandre asked me, 'Did you happen to see the color of their caps?' [A Greek expression indicating that one is driving very fast.] Well, I was forced to say no. We turned around and passed the poor fellows again, at the same breakneck speed. They must've thought we'd missed the racetrack at Le Mans! Frankly, I was scared to death, not because of the way he was driving, since he was an expert, but because he'd forgotten his *glasses* and was practically *blind* without them."

Naturally, Alexandre was stopped time and time again by the police. After closing their eyes to his infractions for many months, they finally had to inform Onassis that if Alexandre didn't calm down a bit they'd be forced to bring him into court. Onassis in turn gave his son a thorough scolding, not forgetting to give the tutor his share of the blame; poor Koutchouvelis never suspected that his pupil was sneaking out for midnight sorties.

Kostas Koutchouvelis had been hired to take care of Alexandre's education at a time when Onassis felt that his business obligations prevented him from undertaking it himself. He thought Kostas (one of his own childhood friends) would be just the right person to teach his son Greek, since Alexandre spoke only French and English to his parents and nurses. Onassis selected the right man; in just six months, Alexandre was fluent, and today, like his father, he speaks almost impeccable Greek, French, Spanish, English and German. Koutchouvelis was also in charge of teaching Alexandre something about life. By the age of fifteen, Alexandre was being taken to cabarets in order to learn to get along with girls. And, of course, he soon found that the fair sex could be a pleasant diversion from his cars. Nicolas and I were in on an adventure involving Alexandre and a certain German girl, which could have been disastrous for all of us.

One night in September, 1965 or '66, the three of us met in front of Alexandre's hotel, the Hermitage (he didn't live on the *Christina* when he was in Monte Carlo), before setting off for a charming and fashionable little nightclub in Cannes. We chose a table and spotted several attractive young hookers sitting at the bar. Alexandre showed a preference for a blonde German girl, who must have been a foot taller than he was. We picked up two other girls and the six of us spent the evening drinking a little, dancing a bit and flirting a lot. By four o'clock we split up into couples and agreed to meet back at the car in an hour's time.

Five o'clock found Nicolas and myself sitting in the front seat of the car with no sign of Alexandre. Fifteen minutes passed, then a half-hour. Still nothing. Nicolas and I began to get very nervous. (We had visions of Alexandre being kidnapped and held for ransom, knowing that whatever happened Onassis would hold us morally responsible.) Frantic, we finally started hunting for him high and low in the streets, as if the German girl might somehow have dumped him behind a nearby lamppost.

Two hours later, absolutely exhausted, we quit our foolish search and decided to return to the car, just as Alexandre wandered up, hands in his pockets, whistling cheerfully.

"Where the hell have you been?" we shouted.

"Cool it," he said. "I did exactly the same thing *you* did—only *six times!*"

Somewhat later, Alexandre went to live with Koutchouvelis in an apartment next to the offices of Olympic Maritime, 17 Boulevard d'Ostende. There he resorted to tying sheets together to make his nightly exits, but after our famous evening we took care not to accompany him on these escapades.

The same year, his father decided to see if his son was capable of handling money. Until then, he hadn't even had an allowance and we were often lending him enough money to buy drinks; this—with the greatest good faith—he promised to pay back when he was rich. Onassis opened a checking account in his name, deposited $14,375, and gave him a checkbook. The first thing Alexandre did with a good portion of the money was to completely outfit himself for "go-carting" and join a carting club in Monaco. Naturally, Onassis soon got wind of this. On the stern of the *Christina,* the millionaire gave his son a tongue-lashing that could be heard all over the ship. Among the many recommendations Onassis made that day, I remember above all hearing him advise his son that he must first learn how to *earn* money before he went about spending it, something which Alexandre found out for himself a few years later. At that time, however, his consuming passion for speed was too much for him and again almost cost him his life when he was spending a vacation on the *Christina.*

Onassis happened to be taking a nap after lunch, when Alexandre asked the first mate, Jean Kefalogianis, to take him out for a spin in the Chris-Craft. Jean agreed. Almost immediately Alexandre asked if he could take the wheel. Jean was a little nervous about letting the boy drive a speedboat that went over forty miles per hour, but he finally gave in to the youngster's incessant pleas. Alexandre was fine for a while until all of a sudden—probably because he got tired of concentrating—he lost control and drove straight into a fishing boat with two men aboard. The Chris-Craft cut the smaller boat neatly in two. Luckily, the fishermen escaped injury and Alexandre was thrown clear, but Kefalogianis was hurled against the smashed boat and required a total of seventy stitches.

There's no need to go into the reception that awaited Alexandre back on the yacht. This time Onassis was really angry. He prohibited his son from any car or boat rides for a very long time and took stern disciplinary measures in many other areas. That accident cost Onassis $30,000, including $15,000 to Kefalogianis, who quit the *Christina* soon afterward.

Today, Alexandre is a mature young man. He has a pilot's license and flies his own planes, but because of his father's business he has very little free time left to devote to his childhood passion for speed. Since 1970, Onassis has spent a great deal of time training Alexandre in the fine points of running his enormous empire, and in addition to the young man's duties toward Olympic Maritime and Olympic Airways, he has twenty ships of his own, which his father gave him for his twentieth birthday. Alexandre will one day be among the richest men in the world.

6 | Scandal and Divorce

The summer of 1959 was to be a period of great change for Onassis. Who could have guessed that at the beginning of August among three dozen guests aboard the *Christina* for a cocktail party you could have found the three most important women in his life: Tina, Maria Callas and Jacqueline Kennedy? Onassis, in fact, was meeting Mrs. Kennedy for the first time at that party. On the other hand, he'd known Maria Callas for some time; she and her husband, Mr. Ménéghini, had been on several cruises before this one, which was to prove so decisive for the famous singer and her host.

Jackie Kennedy was not at all taken with the Greek millionaire, since she was in the process of helping her husband, who was then a senator, plan his Presidential campaign.

Before I describe this historic meeting, and the cruise that followed it, I would like to point out that Onassis was in a particularly bad mood that summer. It turned out that one of his distant cousins, of which he has many, had caused him a great deal of embarrassment.

In any case, Onassis had rather a cynical attitude about his large family, who were in the habit of taking advantage of their rich relative. When a director of Olympic Maritime complained that one of these cousins was stealing outright from the company, Onassis remarked: "My dear fellow, what do you want me to do about it? At least the man isn't destitute. If I fire him and hire another who's really in need, he'll steal *twice* as much from me."

But to continue, Onassis had received from the cousin in question one of those letters full of phrases like: "Ten of us living in one room"; "Nothing but bread and water"; "I beg of you to help us just this once"; "Only your aid can save us from starvation"; "We will be forever grateful." As one might expect, Onassis was deluged with letters of this sort every day, but he took care to consider each one for two reasons. First, he was a basically softhearted man and found it difficult to refuse his own people; but more practically speaking, he wanted to make sure that no overzealous reporter found one of his cousins or uncles living on the charity of the Salvation Army.

Accordingly, when Onassis received this particular plea, he immediately had the cousin added to a list of similar cases to receive an allowance of one hundred eighty dollars a month. This contented his relative for only a few months and soon he decided to set up a garage. He told everybody that his wealthy cousin had ordered him to do some important work and that he needed equipment. Since Onassis is a magic name around Athens, no one hesitated to give him what he needed, especially as the man was crude enough to tell them to send the bills directly to the offices of Olympic Maritime.

At the end of July, Onassis received bills amounting

to $34,000 for equipment he'd never ordered. To avoid a scandal, he paid. But considering his outrage, it was fortunate for this particular cousin that he, too, bore the name Onassis; the boss simply didn't want his family's name sullied in court.

This incident was the primary cause of Onassis' unusually short temper with us that summer. We always had to be on our toes, obeying his least command whenever the ship had to be prepared for a cruise or guests were expected. That year we were setting off for a three-week cruise on August 7. The Churchills had come aboard a few days earlier and had settled in their cabins, as was their custom, when Onassis heard that the Kennedys were vacationing on the Riviera.

After asking Churchill whether he would enjoy meeting John Kennedy (Churchill had known Joe Kennedy in London when he was ambassador to England) and getting a positive response, he extended an invitation to the senator, who accepted with great enthusiasm. The cocktail party was scheduled for August 5.

Meanwhile, Maria Callas and her husband had come from northern Italy to board the yacht, which was anchored at Monte Carlo. This was how Onassis unwittingly managed to assemble in one place his wife (from whom he was to separate only two months later), the woman who was to share his life for the next ten years and the woman who was to become his second wife.

As it turned out, Onassis barely exchanged more than a few words with Jacqueline Kennedy, preferring to talk politics with John and Sir Winston, while no one even thought to introduce Maria Callas to the future First Lady of the United States. Otherwise, the party was very elegant and gay. The Kennedys left at 7:30 P.M.; Jackie was not destined to see Onassis again for the next four years.

On August 7, we left Monte Carlo for Glyfada. Since it was there that Onassis saved me from being thrown into prison, I shall let my own story take over for a moment here before continuing the recital of the important events of the cruise.

Onassis and Churchill had been invited ashore for dinner and so the crew was free to leave the ship from ten o'clock on. The first mate warned us, however, that the last boat back would be at 2 A.M., and, what's more, that the *Christina* was setting off again soon after. To miss the last boat would be fatal.

As luck would have it, I happened to run into a charming and willing girl who invited me up to her place. When I finally left her, I was panicked to discover that it was 2:45 A.M. I ran all the way to the dock, but it was immediately clear that I had no way of getting back to the *Christina*, apart from a police launch sitting there with two officers aboard. In the distance, I could see the glimmering lights of the *Christina*, which was somewhat reassuring.

I approached the two policemen and spoke very casually. "I'm terribly afraid that you'll have to take me out to the *Christina*."

They looked at me as if I was crazy. "We're not here to attract customers," the tall one said. "We're waiting for our chief."

"Don't sweat it," I said coolly. "He's at Zampétas with Mr. Onassis and Mr. Churchill. He's the one who said you'd give me a lift."

After exchanging glances, they seemed convinced

that I was on the level and told me to hop aboard. They even turned on the siren as we sped toward the *Christina.*

Awaiting us at the other end was the first mate, Kostas Andriatos, the only officer still awake at that hour. Not knowing what was happening, he hurriedly straightened his tie and put on his shoes to greet me as I climbed up the ladder. Behind me the two policemen were saluting. While the policemen listened, I calmly explained that my uncle was the chief of police of Glyfada and that since I'd missed the last boat, he had kindly arranged for my return.

Unfortunately, that wasn't the end of the matter. Back on the dock, an important and very angry police chief was waiting for the launch, which was then returning from the *Christina.*

The crowning blow was that we didn't leave as planned anyway, and the *Christina* was still sitting at anchor at 11 A.M., when the two policemen returned for an explanation. They discovered I had no uncle who was chief of police and demanded that I be handed over to the authorities immediately. The problem was that neither the captain, Schlatermund, nor the two policemen could identify me. Of course, the first mate, Andriatos, who was still furious at me because of my fictitious uncle, would've gladly pointed me out, but at the last moment Onassis agreed to speak to the policemen himself.

He argued that an investigation of all sixty members of the crew would delay the *Christina*'s imminent departure. Since there was no other way of discovering the guilty party, he offered to conduct the investigation himself. By this time, the policemen reasoned that it would be better to let the matter drop. As you might expect, I hadn't heard the last of this from my friends, but I had no trouble getting Onassis to understand my dilemma, since Andriatos had assured us the ship was leaving shortly after 2 A.M., and I would certainly have lost my job if the policemen hadn't been so conveniently waiting at the dock.

This incident illustrates, I think, why all of us had complete confidence in Onassis and felt perfectly safe while under his protection. Although we all knew how difficult and demanding he could be, we also realized that he respected each individual.

We finally left Glyfada and headed into the Aegean, because the guests wanted to visit some of the tiny islands around Athens and Thessalonica. The first sign of trouble appeared around the tenth day. The weather had gotten very rough and practically all the guests, plus Tina, her children and Mr. and Mrs. Garoufalides, Onassis' sister and brother-in-law, were sick and were forced to stay in their cabins. Only Maria and Onassis were completely untouched by the storm. All day long they chatted, drank, laughed, danced and listened to music while the boat rolled and tossed on the heavy seas.

Of course, the sickest one of all was Ménéghini, whose condition didn't improve, despite our ministrations. I'm sure the poor man didn't feel any better knowing that while he was flat on his back below deck, his wife was upstairs flirting with her host, who admittedly had paid her a good deal of attention since the very beginning of the cruise. However, I should make one thing clear at this point: Onassis and Maria were indulging in a perfectly harmless flirtation and never once said or did anything that could be interpreted the wrong way. On looking back, it seems to me that Onassis might possibly have been trying to make his wife jealous, since over the past months she had become more and more distant with him.

I might also point out that Tina hadn't wanted to invite *anyone* along on the cruise that summer, perhaps because she hoped to make one last effort to save her marriage.

In any case, things became very uncomfortable when Ménéghini, who had been in bed for forty-eight hours, finally felt well enough to get up. He immediately sensed what had been going on and the two men had a terrible scene in Onassis' office, with the result that Ménéghini declared he was taking his wife off the yacht as soon as they got to Venice; they would not continue the cruise.

Tina, for her part, was much more discreet and acted as if the whole affair had nothing to do with her.

Early in the morning of our arrival in Venice, two boats were launched, one to take the Ménéghinis ashore, the other to satisfy Churchill's desire to tour the canals of Venice.

After an exhausting but satisfying day admiring the palaces of Venice and listening to the singing of gondoliers, the group went out to dinner at a restaurant in the Piazza San Marco. I'd like to stress that during all this time Onassis didn't seem the slightest bit depressed by the abrupt departure of Maria; he continued to laugh and joke with the others.

After a few days' stop in Venice, the *Christina* set out for Naples. But soon after arriving, Onassis and all the guests found it so unpleasant trying to escape from the crowds, photographers and newspapermen, that it was decided to return at once to Monte Carlo.

At this point, events took a turn for the worse, and an almost malicious succession of misunderstandings succeeded in separating Mr. and Mrs. Onassis forever.

First of all, just before leaving Naples, Onassis got a telegram requiring his immediate presence in Paris for business reasons. He apologized to family and friends and took a plane to the French capital.

But the Italian newspapers were already up-to-date on Onassis' flirtation with Maria and his subsequent argument with Ménéghini. (There are always some indiscreet members of the crew who can't resist the bribes offered by newspapermen.) The press interpreted Onassis' departure their own way. Never to be outdone when it comes to scandal, they claimed that Onassis had fled to the woman he now loved. Despite this complete distortion of the facts, the damage was done.

Reading the account in the newspapers, Tina became convinced that she had been duped by her husband. Humiliated and angry, she abandoned the attitude of forbearance that had carried her through the trying days of the cruise. She had finally lost confidence in her husband. After seeing the Churchills off at Monte Carlo, she left the yacht with her children.

Totally unaware of what had happened, Onassis arrived back on the *Christina* the next day and was astonished to find only the crew aboard.

Even then, things could have been straightened out between the couple if Onassis' father-in-law, Livanos, hadn't taken a most unfortunate step. He arrived on the *Christina* to demand an explanation for the scandalous reports in all the newspapers. One thing led to another and soon the two men were in the midst of a terrible argument. After this final confrontation there was only one path Onassis could follow: he set off to win Maria from her husband. He was going to turn the lies into truth and justify the suspicions of Tina, Livanos, Méneghini and the press.

I suppose you have to be named Onassis to attempt to walk off coolly with the woman of your choice from her husband's house. Three days later he was on his way to Italy to try to do just that. When he arrived in front of the Méneghini residence, he had a glass in one hand and a bottle of whiskey in the other. Somewhat drunk, he told Méneghini that he had come to fetch Maria and that he was going to marry her. The two rivals argued for three solid hours. Méneghini repeatedly tried to get Onassis to leave, but to no avail. Maria was nowhere to be seen. Finally, Méneghini relinquished the living room to Onassis and went upstairs to his office. Never easily outdone by the retreat of an enemy, Onassis followed him. After a long search, he accidentally found Maria, shut in her room. She had undoubtedly overheard the entire conversation between Onassis and her husband, but hadn't wanted to interfere.

Onassis took her by the hand and asked to be led to her husband's office for one final meeting. When they found him, he was sound asleep on his bed.

"I just told your husband that I'd come to take you away," he said, appalled. "The only effect it had was to put him to sleep!"

A few minutes later, Maria left her home and the

man who had helped her become the greatest opera singer in the world. They spent several days at Onassis' apartment in Paris before setting off on a second cruise, the beginning of a stormy but passionate relationship that was to last almost ten years.

7 | Maria Callas

Many intimate friends of Onassis were very unhappy over Ari's separation from his wife and his subsequent affair with Maria. Lady Churchill, for example, had been very fond of Tina and later came aboard the *Christina* only with great reluctance.

Prince Rainier and Princess Grace of Monaco strongly disapproved of the publicity caused by the affair and as a result their business relations suffered. Nevertheless, Onassis had an idea which could have transformed Monte Carlo into a haven for music lovers, a center very much like Salzburg in Austria. He planned to build a magnificent opera house so that Maria could not only give exclusive recitals, but also serve as musical director of the center. Unfortunately, this dream never became reality, primarily because, as everyone knows, Maria preferred to devote more time to her new companion than to her career.

When the cruise was over, Maria went to live at Onassis' Paris apartment on the Avenue Foch. George and Hélène were clearly enthusiastic about their new mistress, whose outstanding characteristics were understanding and kindness. When she went shopping for herself, she always brought back a present for her servants. She was always courteous and appreciated all the hard work that went into maintaining the apartment.

George and Hélène were particularly touched when she even had a special refrigerator installed near the bedrooms so that when she and Onassis came in late, as they often did, they wouldn't awaken the two servants, who slept right next to the kitchen.

Maria also took great interest in all aspects of Onassis' life. She told him early in their relationship that it was ridiculous to pay the crew of the *Christina* overtime, since they could just as easily take extra time off at a later date.

I must say this idea didn't appeal to us very much, since our salaries were not all that generous. But I have to admit that from a business point of view, Maria was right; there just wasn't a great deal of work to be done aboard the *Christina*, except during cruises.

I remember the time Maria had an argument with Charlie, the bartender (Charlie had by now replaced Louis) because he wasn't respectful enough to her. This was the first time Maria had ever spoken sharply to a servant and she was absolutely right to do so; Charlie sometimes needed to be taken down a notch or two. Unlike Tina, Maria wanted to be in on all aspects of running the *Christina*. For example, she loved to come into the galley just before dinner to see how things were going. This nearly drove the cook, Clément Miral, out of his mind, since Maria would always lift the cover of the main dish, dip in a piece of bread and sample it.

"There'll be hell to pay," Clément used to say, "if

the boss finds a piece of bread in the sauce. What excuse can I possibly give him? That it's the fault of his new *mistress?*"

Maria normally ate almost nothing except fruit and yogurt, although she loved to eat. Many people have wondered how she managed to lose so much weight in the early 1950s. This was a secret even Onassis didn't know until a nearly fatal evening in 1965 when he ended up saving the singer's life.

One night he received a frantic phone call from Maria, who then lived a few doors away on the Avenue Foch. She was in agonizing pain. Onassis rushed over to find her deathly pale, courageously trying to endure the racking pain in her stomach, but unable to explain what was the matter. He implored Bruna, her maid, to tell him the whole story. Finally, convinced that her mistress was in great danger, the servant confessed that Maria had had a tapeworm for many years. Although her doctor had given her appropriate medicine, she had refused to take it for fear of gaining weight again. So at that very moment, Maria was on the verge of an intestinal rupture.

Onassis' rage at this news can scarcely be imagined. Swearing up and down that everyone in this crazy world was out of their minds, he called his English doctor, had a plane sent from Orly to pick him up, and had the physician at Maria's bedside a few hours later. After the crisis had passed, Onassis couldn't help but read her the riot act for her idiotic behavior.

This might be a good place to point out that throughout the ten years of their life together, Onassis and Maria continued to have frequent arguments, separations and reconciliations. But never, in all this time, did they have a fight in front of the servants (which is not to imply that everything they said couldn't be *heard* by the servants, owing to Onassis' thundering voice). In view of this, Maria developed a system to avoid confrontations altogether. Whenever she sensed Onassis' increasing wrath was about to explode, she would station herself somewhere on the ship where she was sure to be in the presence of servants. Her first choice was the galley. This naturally made everyone nervous, knowing that another storm was brewing between the boss and the famous singer.

In these instances, Onassis never followed Maria, but after a while, when he'd calmed down, he used the intercom to call the galley and ask if Madame was there. He then asked that she be invited to rejoin him, the signal that the storm had passed.

Of course, at other times it was Onassis who walked out, but he never took refuge in the galley. Instead, he would go to a fashionable restaurant, usually Maxim's, or to a nightclub near St. Germain des Prés. Sometimes he would even take an Olympic flight to Athens, then a car to Glyfada, so he could go to Zampétas with his sister and brother-in-law to dance and—for a few hundred dollars extra—break some plates and glasses. Once he even broke a chair.

One of Maria's friends happened to be at Zampétas during one of Onassis' most violent rages, when he ran up a "damage" bill of eighteen hundred dollars. The friend immediately called Maria and asked what in hell was going on between the two of them. "If this continues," she said, "Ari's going to set fire to all of Athens!"

The next day Onassis returned to Paris and lunched

with Maria, whom he had invited to his apartment. The fight broke out again, this time over his excesses at Zampétas. Finally, her patience exhausted, the singer got up and started to throw everything on the Persian rug, including the oil, grape leaves and wine. When there was nothing left for her to toss around or break, she went home.

But Maria didn't stay in this mood for very long. Her usual practice was to go home, unplug the telephone and shut herself in her room, after telling all of her servants that she never wanted to see Onassis again. By the time evening rolled around, she'd reattach the phone and replace her key under the doormat where Onassis was accustomed to finding it.

Maria did manage once to hold out until almost midnight. Onassis, not being able to get her on the phone, arrived to find the door locked and the key gone. Undaunted, he went out and started to whistle underneath her window. Getting no response, he started to call her name, his voice growing louder and louder. Finally, he told her that if she didn't let him in, he was going to get his car and smash the door. Frightened by this threat, she threw him the key. Later, she rationalized her capitulation by telling her maid that she had only given in because they would've become the laughingstock of the entire world if a newspaperman had happened by at the time.

On another occasion, Onassis even went on a hunger strike after one of their arguments. It was Christmas time and he'd just returned from a tiring business trip in New York. For some reason, he started to argue with his son Alexandre. Maria made the mistake of joining in and said that Alexandre didn't seem very happy anyway, probably because he didn't get enough attention and affection from his father.

I might mention here that Alexandre never really forgave Maria for replacing his mother in his father's affections. He tried to avoid taking vacations on Skorpios or the *Christina* when she was there, and even made an effort not to be in the same room with her if he could help it. He was, of course, too young to realize that long before Maria came along his parents had ceased to be compatible and that the singer really had very little to do with their final decision to separate. But despite this resentment, which prevented Maria and Alexandre from developing a close relationship, she often took the boy's side against Onassis.

So in this instance, exasperated by the less than warm reception he had expected to receive, Onassis shut himself in his room for an entire week and would speak to no one, except to order a bowl of soup a day. Maria took the opportunity to go on a diet of strawberries and yogurt. Meanwhile, Alexandre was left to spend a very dismal Christmas in the kitchen with the butler and his wife.

Despite his appearance as the hardheaded businessman, Onassis was often overcome with a need for tenderness and brooded that no one liked him for himself. He is, in fact, extremely sentimental, as demonstrated by an occasion when he was so tortured by insecurity that he actually threatened to disinherit his son.

It seems Alexandre announced to his father that in spite of all his toys and his wonderful stereo set, he was bored. He wanted to spend some time with his mother and sister, to have friends to play with, to be more like other boys with ordinary fathers. And he was tired of being bombarded with questions about his father and being photographed wherever he went.

Onassis hit the ceiling. He was in the process of making the painful discovery that his son was *not* the happiest child in the world—but with all his business obligations, he couldn't do anything about it. And so, when Alexandre concluded by asking if he could visit his mother for a few days, Onassis said in no uncertain terms that he was going to disinherit him. Of course, he loved his son too much to have ever carried out this threat, but in those days Alexandre pretended not to care about money and made that fact abundantly clear to his father. Again, it was Maria who came to the rescue and persuaded Onassis to be reasonable.

One of the greatest problems faced by this unusual couple was how to maintain their privacy. They always waited until nightfall to come into port on the *Christina,* and a Chris-Craft without lights deposited them ashore as discreetly as possible. They never went to fashionable restaurants where photographers might be lurking, and they tried to enter hotels via the service entrance. In view of all these precautions, I must relate a charming adventure that befell the couple in 1964, the result this time of Maria's extraordinary popularity.

One day in Naples, Maria asked Onassis to take her to Mount Vesuvius so they could climb to the top. This they did. As they returned to the foot of the mountain after a long and wonderful walk, they were greeted by a very old Italian couple standing on the threshold of their dilapidated house. Timidly approaching Maria, they told her they had always admired her singing and that in spite of their poverty they had managed to buy practically all of her recordings. They concluded by asking the singer and her friend (they had no idea who he was) to share their simple afternoon meal. Onassis, seeing Maria hesitate, instantly accepted the invitation and the four of them sat down to a feast of macaroni and cheese. To celebrate, Onassis ordered a couple of bottles of champagne brought up from the yacht.

This meal really meant more to Onassis than the most expensive gift, since it was offered out of appreciation for the great talent of Maria Callas and had nothing to do with his money.

This is an appropriate place to mention that Maria was one of the few people who absolutely never took advantage of Onassis' wealth. She rarely accepted gifts from him, much as he wanted to spoil her. Once he offered to give her two thousand dollars a month, which he had discreetly ascertained was the expense of her house and servants, but she flatly refused.

Perhaps even more remarkable is the fact that Onassis, who was not in the habit of taking advice from women, listened to Maria, who told him her opinion on virtually every subject. In addition, Maria often accompanied him to business dinners where, with feminine intuition and her own great intelligence, she would offer rather shrewd advice.

Her greatest challenge was to prevent the crew from stealing. With the exception of the old and faithful retainers, most of the men were neither very bright nor very honest. I'm not talking about the officers, who couldn't have been more devoted, but about those fellows who only worked for a few months at a time. They were often bored to death on the *Christina*, where the only treat available while at anchor was a glass of ouzo at the café on Lefkas.

Maria understood this situation perfectly and therefore paid great attention to the newcomers, making sure that a thief didn't go off with one of the valuable paintings or objets d'art in Onassis' collection. For almost ten years, she served as his private detective as well as a perfect "wife." In return, Maria had the complete respect of everyone who ever worked for her.

After that famous cocktail party in 1959, when she observed Jacqueline Kennedy in action for the first time, Maria had several other encounters with the First Lady of the United States.

Their second meeting was in 1963, shortly before the death of John Kennedy. It happened in a rather roundabout way. During his numerous travels, Onassis had an opportunity to meet Jackie's sister Lee Radziwill and they became fast friends. Unfortunately, the friendship developed to such an extent that gossip insisted it was much more than that. In truth, Lee was very happy with Prince Radziwill, and Onassis was completely content with Maria.

But, of course, in those days it was only necessary for a woman to smile at Onassis to start the tongues wagging and supply juicy tidbits for the scandal sheets. Maria knew this. And although Onassis' friendship with the princess didn't exactly delight her, she remained silent.

Early in 1963, Princess Radziwill told Onassis that things were not going very smoothly between her sister and John Kennedy. In fact, as was widely rumored a few years later, the couple were on the brink of separation and the only thing that held them together was pressure from Joe Kennedy, who understood that a break would permanently damage his son's political career.

Onassis thought that if he offered his hospitality to Jackie for a while it might enable the couple to make it through this difficult period, which the Kennedy clan considered merely temporary.

"Why not ask Jackie to join us on a two-week cruise aboard the *Christina?*" he suggested.

Lee thought it was an excellent idea and immediately relayed the invitation to her sister.

Jackie was enthusiastic about the trip, but she had a hard time getting her husband to agree to such a long separation. However, she insisted so strenuously that John Kennedy finally gave in.

The *Christina* sailed with three guests: Jackie, Lee and Maria. In order to avoid publicity, it was announced that Onassis would not be aboard. He also took precautions not to show himself while in port, but spent the rest of the time happily with his guests. As usual, the press discovered the truth. About a week into the cruise, an Italian photographer who happened to be in Greece succeeded in taking a picture of Onassis with a telephoto lens. Thus, it was disclosed once and for all that he was in fact aboard with the rest. But who would have suspected at the time that like a simple peasant girl the First Lady of the United States was falling in love with Onassis?

The first person who realized that Jackie was in love with Onassis, aside from Maria Callas, was John Kennedy himself. Maria didn't take it very seriously, since it seemed unlikely to her that Jackie would divorce the President.

In a letter that quite a few people at the White

House saw at the time, Jackie described Onassis with such uncharacteristic enthusiasm that John Kennedy asked her, by return mail, to come home as soon as possible. In the meantime, he added, his wife should tell him a little less about "this man Onassis," and a little more about Caroline. Jackie calmly continued her cruise all the way to Turkey, but took care not to mention Onassis in subsequent letters to her husband.

At that time, the idea of a love affair or even a great friendship between Jackie and Onassis seemed highly improbable. In spite of his hundreds of millions of dollars, he simply didn't belong to the same social class as Jackie. Yet, as many have known since 1968, and as I myself guessed in 1964, these two people were destined to one day become man and wife.

Even if John Kennedy hadn't been assassinated, I personally think Jackie would have divorced him and most certainly married Onassis.

The words of General de Gaulle come to mind, as recorded in that wonderful book André Malraux wrote about him: "She [Jackie] is a brave and cultivated woman, but as for her future, you are deceived. I can see her on the yacht of a Greek oil shipping magnate."

But not to get ahead of ourselves, let's go back to this cruise of 1963. It was obvious that Jackie and Maria were not to become the best of friends. A few days before leaving the yacht, Jackie invited Maria to the White House, just as she had often invited other great artists. The singer courteously but firmly refused. The die was cast.

When Jackie returned to the United States with her daughter, she knew she had yet another serious admirer; this time, one who didn't leave her altogether indifferent. Someone, in fact, who she hoped to see again as soon as possible.

The next time that Jackie (by then a widow) officially saw Onassis was five years later during another cruise, which took place in the Bahamas. Once again Lee and Maria were aboard, as well as their two servants, and Onassis' sister and brother-in-law, Mr. and Mrs. Garoufalides. But this time the situation was a little more obvious. Just as he had five years earlier, Onassis flirted openly with one of his guests: not Maria, but Jackie. His attraction to her was so blatant that Maria, outraged, took a plane from the Bahamas to New York and then the same day left for Paris.

After Maria was gone, everyone joked about Onassis' true feelings and even organized a "truth" game in order to find out his real sentiments about Jackie; they were anxious to know if he might eventually be tempted to marry the young widow.

I have it from a reliable source that Jackie, when taxed by Lee and Mrs. Garoufalides about why she didn't marry Onassis, replied simply: "He hasn't asked me."

This was the beginning of February, 1968. Two days later, Onassis proved that he was still in love with the woman who had devoted so many years of her life to him. He deserted his guests and followed Maria to Paris.

Reunited in his apartment, the couple made a very serious decision. For the first time since she had shared his life, Maria insisted that he marry her. Among other things, she told him that it would soon be too late for her to have children, a long-cherished dream she didn't intend to sacrifice.

Onassis replied without hesitation: "All right, let's get married."

Maria had won. She was to become Mrs. Onassis. Practically speaking, however, she was still married to Ménéghini, at least according to Italian law. However, she asked for and obtained a divorce in Athens in 1967.

The wedding was scheduled to be held in London during the first week of March. Onassis left Paris with his maid Hélène and settled in the Savoy Hotel. To avoid publicity, Maria took a suite at Claridges. The wedding was set for a few days after their arrival. The witnesses were to be two directors of Olympic Maritime, and a Greek Orthodox priest was ready to fly in from Athens to officiate. Unfortunately, Maria lacked one important document—her birth certificate—and I believe she had to wait two weeks for it.

In the meantime, she busied herself over a lawsuit she was bringing against the shipper Panaghis Vergottis, to whom she had entrusted the use of a ship she had purchased on the advice of Onassis. She maintained that the vessel didn't bring in enough money. At the same time, she quietly ordered her dressmaker to create a dozen new dresses, including a light-beige suit for her wedding.

Finally, it was only a few hours before the ceremony, the plane had left for Athens to pick up the priest and all was in readiness. Then, suddenly, the bride and bridegroom had a violent argument that caused them to break up forever. Onassis immediately left his hotel and took a plane to Athens. Maria returned sadly to Paris.

In Greece, Onassis promptly went to see his family and consulted with them about the possibility of marrying Jackie Kennedy. His family advised him to go ahead. He left for New York, met with Jackie and asked for her hand in marriage.

The wedding was to take place four months later, in July, but the tragedy in Los Angeles that cost Bobby Kennedy his life caused it to be postponed until October.

And while everyone was talking about marriage in New York, Maria Callas in Paris was telling her friends that her favorite opera was Bellini's *Norma.* Rather than continue to annoy her lover, the heroine of this tragedy commits suicide.

8 | The Incredible Marriage

By the beginning of 1968, some time had passed since I left the service of Onassis. Thanks to an inheritance which I wasn't expecting, I suddenly found myself in possession of a fortune. I bought a house in Monte Carlo and I have a rather healthy bank account, enough to live in relative luxury for the rest of my life.

And so, with time on my hands and many exciting memories, I decided to write a biography of my ex-boss that would include all the people who are—or were—among his closest friends.

Many people before me have tried to re-create the fantastic life of this man. In general, they haven't succeeded. For example, I remember an American writer who spent months traveling between Greece, Monte Carlo and Paris in order to collect the necessary information for his book. It was wasted effort, simply because very few of Onassis' present or former employees would even think of discussing the man's private life with a stranger. There are two very good reasons for this. First, most of us genuinely like Onassis and are afraid that what we say might be changed or romanticized. And second, most of his servants are in awe of him and simply don't want to displease him and lose their jobs.

Fortunately, I don't have those problems. From the day I decided to write about Onassis, nothing could have stopped me in the quest for information. I want to make it clear, though, that all the people who spoke to me did so of their own free will; they were not paid. In Monte Carlo and New York, as well as in Greece, I think tongues were loosened merely by the pleasure of being able to add stories and details to my own recollections.

I also want to emphasize that I consider myself very lucky not to be in the service of Jacqueline Onassis. As you'll shortly see, she's not exactly easy to please.

As everyone knows, Onassis married Jacqueline Kennedy on October 20, 1968. But what very few people know is that Jackie had been contemplating this marriage over a period of four years. She felt that only one man was worthy of becoming her second husband: Aristotle Onassis. Very few people are also aware that between 1963 and 1968 the couple in fact saw each other very frequently.

A week before Christmas, 1964, Onassis was in Paris. He summoned his servants George and Hélène and told them that a very important person was scheduled to visit him on December 21. Since the guest had to remain anonymous at all costs, it would be necessary for them to organize their work so that neither of them would actually see the visitor.

George and Hélène were used to their employer's wild flights of fancy, but this time he seemed to be asking the impossible. They racked their brains to think of some way to wait on his friend without ever seeing him—or her. Was someone going to blindfold them and guide them in and out of the room? Eventually, they reported back to their boss to tell him they were stymied. After long thought, Onassis found a solution. He had a revolving table placed in the corridor between the kitchen and the dining room. Hélène could put out the meals, course by course, and Onassis himself would serve them. Next, Hélène was to clean the bedroom reserved for the VIP and make the bed while the guest was in the bathroom; the bathroom could then be cleaned after the guest returned to the bedroom. Both servants were then to remain in the kitchen for the rest of the day.

But there was a third servant who couldn't help but see this mystery guest: Rozas, the chauffeur. On December 21, at exactly eleven o'clock in the morning, he picked up Onassis in the Rolls-Royce and drove him to Orly. At the airport, he was instructed to drive right onto one of the runways, toward an Olympic Airways jet that had just landed. It was a regularly scheduled flight, but only one passenger was aboard: Jackie Kennedy. She was ushered into the car with Onassis, and Rozas headed straight back to Paris. The formality of clearing customs had been waived.

Jackie stayed in his apartment from December 21 to 23. Everything went according to plan and the service was as discreet as possible. But of course George and Hélène knew perfectly well who was visiting their employer.

Whenever Onassis took Jackie out, they never went anywhere they might possibly be recognized. For the most part, they spent their time in one of the living rooms in front of the fireplace. But despite these precautions, there was one incident that could have spoiled the whole visit.

Naturally, Onassis was particularly careful to conceal Jackie's presence from Maria Callas. Accordingly, he told her he had to go away for a few days on business. But on the evening of December 23, when Maria was driving home along the Avenue Foch, she happened to see the Rolls entering his building. Delighted that he had come back early from his business trip, she decided to visit him right away. It was nine o'clock.

Onassis was on the fifth floor where he was busy loading Jackie's suitcases into the elevator, just prior to getting in himself and going down to the garage. The car was ready to drive her back to Orly. Meanwhile, on the ground floor, Maria kept pressing the elevator button but to no avail. Finally deciding it was out of order, she started up the stairs. On the fourth floor she caught sight of Onassis for an instant, just as the windowed elevator was passing. Luckily, she didn't see the person behind him. In the time it took her to get all the way down to the garage, the Rolls was already speeding down the Avenue Foch.

When he returned about an hour later, Onassis found Maria sitting calmly in front of the television in his living room. She mentioned that she had seen him in the elevator, but from her tranquil expression he knew that she suspected nothing. He merely apologized for not having stopped, telling her the truth—he just hadn't seen her. Thus the incident was closed without a scene.

Jackie returned three months later and the same procedures were followed, only this time Onassis decided to invite a third person to one of their intimate lunches at the apartment, his son Alexandre. The young man was quite surprised to find himself in the presence of the former First Lady of the United States. But he was accustomed by then to expect almost anything from his father and made an effort to be sociable. The lunch went off very well. Later, he asked George and Hélène: "What the hell is my father doing with Jackie Kennedy?"

Considering that Jackie came from Washington especially to see Onassis on these two occasions, one naturally wonders exactly how far the relationship had progressed at that point. It was something of an enigma to those few who were aware of Jackie's secret visits. Did Onassis have some ulterior business motive in getting to know her because of her valuable contacts? Were they simply good friends? Or were they lovers? The most one can say is that they were strongly attracted to each other. Almost certainly Onassis wasn't ready to marry Jackie; he was still in love with Maria. Jackie finally came to terms with this fact in 1966.

Counting her trips to Paris and Onassis' visits to Washington and New York, they had seen each other at least thirty times since the death of John Kennedy. But in all that time, he had never broached the subject of marriage. For this reason, at the beginning of 1966, Jackie resumed the active social life she had abandoned after Dallas and decided at the same time to stop seeing Onassis. And she didn't see him again until the famous cruise that sealed their fate in January, 1968.

I hardly think it's necessary to repeat the details of the marriage ceremony, which, thanks to extensive coverage in the press, are familiar to everybody. On the other hand, few people know anything about the unusual marriage contract written by the couple's attorneys and signed in New York on October 17, 1968, three days before their wedding.

I'm not at liberty to say how I happened to see a copy of this contract, but I'd like to point out a few of the more unusual clauses. As you'll see, Aristotle Onassis and Jacqueline Kennedy aren't people who engage lightly in the business of life, particularly when marriage is concerned.

In the early days of their marriage, a great many newspapers voiced the suspicion that Jackie was pregnant. A look at Clause Twenty-three shows that this would have been virtually impossible: Jacqueline Bouvier Kennedy agreed to marry Aristotle Onassis on the express condition that he did not require her to give him a child. Aside from the time she was required to spend with her husband (see Clause Seven below), Jackie insisted on devoting all of her energy to her children Caroline and John-John. There was never any question, therefore, of her having a third child.

Furthermore, Jackie declared that she wished to retain a great deal of her freedom. Under Clause Seven, she agreed to spend only Catholic holidays and summer vacations with her new husband. For the rest of the year, she reserved the right to travel alone and to visit her friends and family without asking her husband's permission.

In my opinion, Clause Nineteen is perhaps the most remarkable of all. It stipulates that Onassis and Jackie will always sleep in separate bedrooms, which explains why she has her own house on Skorpios and why she sleeps in the luxurious cabin on the *Christina* that used to be the exclusive domain of her husband. He was relegated to one of the guest rooms on a deck below, a cabin that bears the name Lesbos. In New York, Jackie lives in her own apartment at 1040 Fifth Avenue, while Onassis rents (by the year) a suite on the top floor of the Pierre Hotel.

Naturally, a large section of the marriage contract deals with money matters. Here, details about Jackie's own property and income cover a mere page and a half. In contrast those clauses concerning Onassis cover twenty-seven pages, including specifics about all the companies, properties, possessions and assets of this man, who is among the richest in the world.

It's a fact that Jackie wasn't really a wealthy woman before the marriage. Aside from her New York apartment, a summer house in New Jersey and the capital inherited from John Kennedy (most of which goes to her children), she had very few assets. Therefore, the section on money was designed to cover every contingency.

Suppose, for example, Onassis decides to leave his wife. He must automatically give her $10,000,000 for each year of their marriage. On the other hand, if Jackie leaves Ari before five years of marriage, she'll receive only $20,000,000 in total. However, if she leaves him after five years, she'll still receive the same $20,000,000, but in addition, she'll be entitled to an allowance of $180,000 a year for the next ten years.

If Onassis dies while Jackie's still his wife, she'll inherit $100,000,000 outright, while the rest of his fortune —which must be at least six times that—will go to his children Christina and Alexandre.

If Jackie dies before her husband, all of her possessions go to her children, who will continue to be supported by Onassis until they're twenty-one years of age.

If both husband and wife die before the children are twenty-one, they'll be entrusted to Prince and Princess Radziwill.

Presently, Jackie receives $5,000 a month for her children's education, clothing, nurses and medical bills, and will continue to do so until they are of age.

Jackie herself is also well supported. All the expenses of her New York apartment, taxes, staff, bills, plus the maintenance of her cars, are paid for directly by Onassis' New York secretary. These basic items average approximately $10,000 a month. However, this is far from enough to cover her personal expenses. To pay for her own doctors, masseurs, hairdressers, cosmeticians, pedicurists, and so on, she receives another $7,000 a month. An additional $10,000 a month is allowed for new clothes. And last but not least, she receives $6,000 a month to pay for her personal bodyguards. Two New York private detectives usually accompany her wherever she travels in the world.

When Jackie doesn't travel on Olympic Airways or in her husband's private plane, she's entitled to purchase six first class tickets, since she insists on the following arrangements: the seat beside her, plus the seats directly in front and in back of her, must always be empty; the two seats across the aisle to her right must always be occupied by the two detectives. This would mean that each time Jackie flew from New York to Athens, for example, on an airline other than Olympic, she would spend a total of $6,996 in first class round-trip tickets. Naturally, she flies Olympic whenever possible, because her tickets are free.

In summary, we can conclude from the marriage contract that Jackie, with her children, costs her husband approximately $450,000 a year, which still doesn't take into account the extravagant presents Onassis gives her, nor does it cover the incredible expenses of their daily life, whether they happen to be in Greece, Paris or New York.

To acquire a logical perspective about some of their other major expenses, remember that the *Christina* alone costs $420,000 a year for maintenance, salaries and cruises; and expenses to operate the island of Skorpios come to $365,000 a year. Perhaps the most surprising fact to emerge from all this is that despite the enormous sums of money Onassis spends on his wife and family, he tries every so often to economize in the most ridiculous ways. This habit usually throws Jackie into a rage.

I know of a particular instance when Onassis had a bottle of perfume flown in from Paris in 1969. They were on Skorpios in February of that year. One morning when Jackie was already in a foul mood because her maid spilled a spot of tea on her pink silk sheets, she herself dropped an entire bottle of perfume. The precious liquid spilled all over the carpet. At the end of her tether, Jackie went to see her husband, who happened to be talking to the gardener. She asked him to send somebody to Paris to buy her a new bottle of Chanel No. 5.

Since they were going back to New York in a couple of days, Onassis phoned his servant in Paris and instructed him to buy the medium-size bottle and put it on a regular flight to Athens. A few hours later, when the hydroplane arrived with the package, Jackie and her husband had a terrible fight—because he hadn't bought her the large-size bottle!

When Jackie is displeased, she either pouts or snaps at everybody in a tone of voice that would make you cringe. After the initial rage is over, she invariably goes to her room and shuts herself in for the rest of the day.

On this occasion, she finished with a disgusted shrug of her shoulders. "Thank you for the tiny bottle of perfume," she snapped. "What a big trip for such a small present."

Before Onassis had time to reply, she had disappeared for the rest of the day. I'm sure that if she had been the type of employer to give presents to her servants, she would have disposed of the bottle right then and there, just to annoy her husband.

Virtually everyone I know who's ever been in the service of Jacqueline Kennedy Onassis agrees that she's the most difficult and demanding mistress they ever worked for. To illustrate, Hélène told me the story of Jackie's official arrival in Paris at the end of November, 1968, right after the honeymoon.

In New York, Onassis told Jackie that they were going to spend a little time in Paris with the children. She grudgingly agreed to come, complaining that she and her children didn't feel safe in Paris. Moreover, she added, the entire capital would know of their presence and she had a horror of reporters. She insisted, in any case, that she would only come with her bodyguards.

Onassis tried very hard to convince her that this was unnecessary, arguing that during her previous visits in 1964 and 1965 she had had no trouble. Jackie reminded him that France was no longer the same since the uprising of May, 1968; she simply wouldn't go unless she was fully protected. Onassis had no choice but to give in, and Nancy Tuckerman, Jackie's secretary, was given the job of organizing the trip and notifying the French authorities of Jackie's arrival.

Onassis preceded his wife to Paris by forty-eight hours. On November 27, he was waiting in his apartment when Jackie made her grand entrance around eight o'clock in the evening. To his utter bewilderment, she was accompanied by no less than twelve people. In addition to Caroline and John-John, she had brought her American maid, two Secret Service men, four private detectives and three French policemen.

Before she even had a chance to kiss her husband, the six American men dashed past her into the apartment and made a thorough search of all the rooms. When they finished, the field was clear for the three Frenchmen, who contented themselves with a casual check of the premises.

The men then distributed themselves as follows: one French policeman, one Secret Service man and one detective were placed at the entrance of the building itself; two others were stationed on the landing in front of the door to the apartment; two others were to guard the back entrance. This left two men, a Secret Service man and a detective, who were ordered by Jackie to stay inside the apartment and to sleep outside her bedroom.

It's hardly necessary to be well acquainted with Onassis to imagine his reaction to this invasion. Jackie hadn't been there more than half an hour before he asked her quietly to please accompany him into the next room for a talk. But the ensuing discussion was anything but quiet. No one in the apartment could have failed to hear Onassis' thundering voice.

"Are you completely out of your *mind?* Is this the kind of life you want us to lead?"

"I don't feel *safe* in Paris!" Jackie screamed. "I've got to be *protected!* I won't be able to *sleep!*"

Eventually, she came out into the hall, pale and trembling. Onassis, still in a towering rage, stormed out of the apartment, slammed the door behind him, and didn't come back until very late that night.

On his return he found the army of guards comfortably ensconced in his armchairs, which they'd hauled out into the hall for the night, camping luxuriously, as it were, on conquered territory.

The apartment had been virtually transformed into a third-rate hotel. The policemen slept in shifts in two bedrooms where they had set up cots, and the kitchen became a cafeteria where anyone could eat at any time. Worse still, Jackie had coldly informed Hélène that she, her children and her retinue would eat nothing except spaghetti, steak and milk.

Onassis' anger didn't abate. Every time he made a move in his own apartment, he was greeted by the beatific smile of a lethargic policeman. Moreover, he was besieged by his neighbors, who were outraged that the guards at the door should *search* them—not to mention their friends—every time they came in or went out! Even his servants (who God knows were devoted to him) started to complain that Madame was absolutely impossible.

Hélène was the one who suffered most. Jackie told her that she need no longer make their beds, since her American maid was entrusted with this duty. So after fifteen years of loyal service, Hélène was made to feel like an outsider. Nor did she have less work as a result of this edict. Hélène confided to me that Madame was the most disorderly person imaginable. On the average, Jackie completely changed her clothes four times a day, and before each change she tried on dozens of dresses with different combinations of stockings and underwear. She casually dropped these garments on the floor wherever she happened to be. Hélène had to follow her step by step to put everything away again, since she always became furious if she found anything out of place. Every time she took a bath, she used no less than a dozen towels, which somehow still didn't prevent her from dripping a little water wherever she went. But the real trial for Hélène was taking care of the famous sheets.

Jackie never travels without at least twelve pairs of pink silk sheets, hand embroidered by a group of nuns in an Italian convent. She'll never sleep twice in the same sheets; even if she's only taken a nap in the afternoon, the bed has to be changed before evening. As if this weren't enough work in itself, they had to be hand laundered and meticulously ironed, since Madame wouldn't tolerate the slightest wrinkle. For this job alone, Hélène estimated that she had to allow at least three hours a day.

Jackie was equally fussy about her cosmetics, which she carried in an enormous red leather suitcase. When she reached her destination, they all had to be set out on her dressing table, arranged according to size and manufacturer. She had more than thirty jars of various creams and liquids, five bottles of perfume, six different deodorants and dozens of big combs, little combs, makeup brushes and hairbrushes.

All the women who've ever worked for her told me

the same thing: Jackie's so nervous that she always gives the impression she's about to bite somebody's head off. So, as you can judge, the former First Lady of the United States was hardly an easy woman to work for, and those who had been with Onassis for many years didn't greet her official arrival in Paris with much enthusiasm.

By the third day of this siege, Onassis could stand it no longer and a second battle flared up. It didn't last long, since Jackie usually started to tremble uncontrollably the minute he yelled at her and went immediately to her room. Her behavior was in marked contrast to that of both Maria Callas and Tina, neither of whom were afraid of his wrath and often didn't even bother to answer him when he was in this mood.

On this particular occasion, Jackie stayed in her room for the next two days, which couldn't have pleased the servants more, since the sulking fits of Madame afforded them a semivacation for a day or two.

The subject of the argument was the apartment. Jackie complained because her husband hadn't redecorated the place for her arrival, and to tell the truth, she had a point. As I've mentioned, Onassis is really only interested in his island and his ships, attaching no importance to houses at all. This accounts for the truly lamentable condition of his Paris apartment.

The building itself is worth $600,000, yet the shabbiness and bad taste of the furnishings is rather shocking. The only room that is newly decorated is his bathroom. It's absolutely enormous because it used to be a bedroom and cost him $75,000 to convert seven years ago. The decor is pink marble and features a partially sunken bathtub with ample room for two, oval mirrors sunk into the walls, and a double sink identical to the one on the *Christina,* with dolphins of gold-plated silver for faucets.

Onassis sleeps to the right of the bathroom in a relatively small room, simply furnished, with a Louis XV bureau, and Jackie's room is on the other side, also done in the style of Louis XV.

But once you step out into the main hall, all pretense of elegance fades. It's painted a nondescript gray and has a black-and-white imitation-marble floor. Enormous mirrors adorn all the walls to cover up the numerous cupboards, and the only light is supplied by lanterns that look as if somebody picked them up from a railroad station around the turn of the century.

But the hardest thing for Jackie to bear is the huge portrait of Tina hanging in one of the sitting rooms. Onassis never had this taken down and Jackie makes a point of giving it a disdainful look and a shrug of her shoulders whenever she has to pass it.

Without going into more detail about the many equally drab rooms, it's obvious that this apartment is a far cry from the luxurious existence taken for granted aboard the *Christina.* Since Jackie had been familiar with the apartment since 1964, she naturally expected that her new husband would make an effort to fix it up. It seemed inexcusable to her that nothing was changed and the portrait of Tina still hung where it always had.

"I'll never be able to *live* in this dump," she told him flatly.

"I'll never be able to live with your God-damn *bodyguards.*"

Jackie's response was to take a stack of fashion magazines and books to her room and shut herself in.

It was Onassis who made the first move toward reconciliation. The morning of the second day, he paid a formal visit to his wife and invited her to dine with him at Maxim's. He succeeded in convincing her to leave her bodyguards behind, which was indeed a triumph.

Every time Jackie goes out, which is no big thing in itself, it's as if she's beginning a whole new chapter in the adventure of getting dressed. First of all, whenever she goes anywhere, even for only a few days, she takes no less than twenty suitcases with her. Five of these are for her underwear, two are reserved for the twelve pairs of sheets, one is devoted to her stockings alone, and two others to shoes. The remaining ten contain her outfits, most of which are by Valentino, her New York couturier.

She never spends less than three hours getting dressed, trying on at least ten outfits before making a final decision. And before the discarded clothes can be put back in the closet, they all have to be sent to the cleaner to be pressed again. Naturally, this job must only be entrusted to the best man in town. (This special person can be found next to the Opera in Paris and on Seventy-first Street in New York.) Jackie is so finicky that she even has her stockings pressed, while every suit or dress that is sent to the cleaner is insured for several hundred dollars, even if it only has to be ironed.

Let me digress a bit here while I'm talking about Jackie's wardrobe. When I was last in Greece, I went to see my old friends aboard the *Christina.* As I told you earlier, one of the main sources of income for these people used to be selling liquor at black-market prices. But certain members of the crew have recently found a more profitable trade. It turns out that there are certain collectors who are interested in obtaining anything that belongs to Jacqueline Kennedy Onassis—personal objects, clothes and especially underwear. These people naturally get in touch with members of the crew and offer them fabulous sums of money for such items. Here are some of the actual prices these things command: three hundred to five hundred dollars for a dress, sweater, pair of shoes or blue jeans; one thousand to two thousand dollars for a piece of underwear. Someone told me that a rich nightclub owner in London bought a sky-blue silk nightgown in 1971 for the charming sum of twelve hundred dollars. The same man (I'm not at liberty to disclose his name) bought practically everything necessary to dress, from head to toe, an inflatable doll that by itself sells for the relatively modest sum of one hundred dollars in New York.

By reporting this, I feel that I am solving many a mystery for Jackie, who must have often wondered why she couldn't find certain belongings. I'm sure she'll be very surprised to hear that one of her bras or a pair of stockings may now be in a country where she herself has never been.

In order to protect the good name of certain employees in the Onassis household, as well as provide a useful tip for the "Jackie collectors," I want to make it clear that this illicit trade is only conducted in Greece, either on Skorpios or aboard the *Christina.*

So, getting back to this November evening in 1968, Jackie was finally ready to dine with her husband at Maxim's. At the restaurant's entrance they were greeted by the doorman, a photographer and a shabbily dressed beggar who hurried up to them and asked for money.

Onassis somewhat summarily cut off the demands of this man and followed Jackie inside. Rozas parked the car next to a lamppost a few yards down the street.

They left Maxim's at midnight, got back in the car, and Rozas pulled away. Suddenly, they heard a terrifying noise of ripping metal from the back of the car. Rozas, of course, wanted to stop immediately to see what was wrong, but Jackie, almost hysterical with fright, ordered him to drive on as fast as possible and not to stop until they were home. Once inside the garage, having jumped almost every red light, they saw that part of the back bumper had been torn off and found a piece of heavy electric wire still hanging from the car.

Jackie made up her mind then and there that someone had been trying to electrocute them. Onassis tried to assuage her fears, but to no avail. Jackie, who had understandably been terrified of cars since the Dallas tragedy and had in fact vowed never to set foot in another convertible, once more insisted on the importance of having bodyguards with her at all times, even for the shortest trips. No real harm came of the incident, but at Onassis' request, the French police investigated the matter and determined that no one had plotted to assassinate the couple. It had only been the beggar; bitter at being turned away by the famous millionaire, he had simply wanted to scare them. Jackie couldn't believe the answer was that simple and for all practical purposes she refused to go out in Paris again.

This is why Onassis dines alone at Maxim's so often and spends evenings at a nightclub on the Left Bank, although on some occasions he can be seen with Maria Callas.

Here is a good opportunity to destroy yet another piece of commonly accepted gossip: that Onassis and Maria had resumed their old relationship. Even at the beginning of 1969, when things were going from bad to worse between Onassis and his wife, it couldn't be assumed that for this reason Onassis took up with Maria again. He had, in fact, tried to see her for two months, but every time he telephoned or went over to her apartment he was told she wasn't there. Finally, in March, after he had sent her flowers time after time, Maria agreed to talk to him, but only on the telephone. In spite of everything, Maria retained a feeling of great friendship for Onassis. She could no longer resist the temptation of seeing him and made a date.

Maria wasn't the least unhappy about the publicity her reconciliation with Onassis received. She knew it could only annoy Jackie, against whom she still harbored a great deal of resentment. Today, you still see Maria and Onassis together from time to time, but it's only for friendship's sake.

Of course, after the incident at Maxim's, things were no better between Jackie and Onassis, as is borne out by an episode that took place at Villefranche. Jackie decided once and for all that she would never again go anywhere without at least two bodyguards. To preserve the peace, Onassis agreed. Therefore, on June 22, 1969, the couple disembarked from a plane in Nice accompanied by their two guards. From there, they were scheduled to drive directly to Villefranche, where the *Christina* was anchored, prior to setting off for Greece. It was 8:30 P.M. and dinner was waiting for them on the yacht. But when the car reached the top of the hill that looks down on the port, Jackie could see dozens of photographers, reporters and spectators waiting for them on the dock. She immediately ordered her husband to turn around and find a small restaurant where they could have dinner quietly until the coast was clear again. Onassis really wanted to get to his ship as soon as possible. He pointed out that it would only take a few moments to embark and that she could surely stand the inconvenience. But Jackie refused. Making a great effort to control his temper, he gave in once again, turned back and stopped at a small restaurant called Chez Marino. He told the owner that he was willing to pay any amount of money, but that he wanted the restaurant closed to other people while he and his wife had dinner in peace. The proprietor agreed. The bodyguards settled themselves outside the door. Meanwhile the chauffeur cruised back and forth between the restaurant and the port, ready to notify them as soon as the crowd dispersed. They had to wait until one o'clock. In the blackest of moods, they boarded the yacht and set off immediately for Skorpios.

I might as well say at this point that Jackie lived in horror of this island. It was John-John who first inadvertently planted the seed of fear in his mother. One day when he had been fishing, he came rushing home with the exciting news that Lefkas, the island opposite, had been half destroyed by an earthquake in 1948. That night, Jackie had a long talk with her husband about this catastrophe. She admitted that she could no longer help being afraid that someday the roof was going to cave in on her. In view of this, she would henceforth sleep on the *Christina.*

When Jackie's in Greece, she lives in virtual isolation. She receives no visits from her New York friends and sees very little of the Onassis family. In fact, she's seen Christina only three times since her marriage to Onassis, and Alexandre only five times. By chance, the youngsters have never been on Skorpios or the yacht when she's been there.

Jackie considers her stays in Greece as beauty cures. A typical day means that she gets up at nine o'clock, drinks a cup of tea and takes a swim. Then she lies in the sun, thumbing through French or American periodicals until noon. She has a light lunch with her husband and children, either on the island or the yacht. In general, she eats a broiled steak and drinks a glass of milk. She absolutely hates Greek food and only pecks at it in order not to offend Onassis when he's prepared the meal himself. In the afternoon, she does exercises or goes sailing with her husband. Then she gets out her brushes to do some painting in her very simple style. Unlike her husband, whose greatest pleasure is to stroll around his island, she never goes for walks. It seems she's afraid of the serpents and scorpions that still inhabit some of the more remote parts of the place.

What's more, she takes absolutely no responsibility in overseeing the administration of the island or the yacht, and she's never more than glanced at the magnificent grounds that surround the houses. As for what goes on aboard the *Christina,* the following story illustrates her total lack of interest.

On the Fourth of July, Jackie decided to cook something particularly American in honor of Independence Day—a cheesecake. But after searching high and low around the ship for quite some time, she finally had to ask her husband where the *galley* was! For months she'd walked back and forth within a few feet of it.

The entire crew of the *Christina* confirmed that Jackie never paid the slightest attention to them. And those who had to be in direct contact with her never dared speak to her. One time, a quartermaster happened to be up on deck taking color photographs of Skorpios. Jackie was lying in the sun, about a hundred feet away. She called him over to ask him what he thought he was doing there. Frightened and stammering badly, he explained that he wanted some pictures of the island to send to his wife and children. Without letting him say another word, she declared that he was obviously taking pictures of her on the sly to sell to the press. She promptly confiscated his camera.

It seems to me that John-John and Caroline are the only ones who are truly happy on Skorpios, where they come for Christmas, Easter and summer vacations. Onassis bought them a little red fishing boat, the *Caroline*, and had some marvelous ponies brought over that they ride for hours at a time. Their favorite pastime, however, is fishing. In this sport, they have a wonderful friend and conspirator in Nikos Kominates, a fisherman and restaurant owner from Lefkas. The Onassises have such faith in Nikos, who takes the youngsters out every day, that they don't even send the bodyguards with them.

Nikos himself told me the important secret about these fishing parties. As a rule the children catch very few fish, if any, but before setting off Nikos hides some of his own catch on the boat for them to bring back to their mother and stepfather. This delights both the parents, and Onassis has even nicknamed John-John "Poseidon."

Both children like their stepfather a great deal and

he does everything he can to make them happy. John-John is really great friends with Onassis and loves to hear him tell fantastic stories of whale hunting. One day the youngster asked if he could be admiral of the Onassis fleet when he grew up.

This might be a good place to point out that Onassis is about as bad a sailor as he is a good businessman. One day in 1969 he decided to take the *Christina II*, a small pleasure boat, out for a sail. He'd only been gone a little while before he completely lost control and ran on the rocks. Luckily, a nearby yacht caught sight of him and came to the rescue. Once safely aboard, he couldn't refrain from telling the captain, "You know, I have a yacht too, only it's a bit bigger than yours."

It really seems as if life should have gone smoothly for the Onassises, since Jackie undoubtedly had everything a woman could reasonably ask for. She was in fact so spoiled by her husband that after the first three years of marriage she had one hundred twenty bracelets (fifty of which contain diamonds), more than one hundred pairs of earrings, three hundred necklaces and close to one thousand rings. On top of this, she had an extraordinary collection of precious stones that Onassis picked up here and there in his travels.

Onassis' favorite jewelers are Van Cleef & Arpels in New York and Zolotas in Athens. Bills from these two stores come into the offices of Olympic Airways. They show that he buys no less than $20,000 worth of jewels for his wife every month. The most extravagant gift he ever had made for Jackie was a pair of bedroom slippers that he ordered specially from Zolotas for her birthday in August, 1970. A diamond of sixteen karats adorns the center of each slipper and the rest of the blue velvet creations are studded with smaller diamonds and emeralds, in a design of circles and triangles. The slippers cost $120,000.

You would think that Onassis could scarcely provide another thing to make his wife happy. But I happen to know that Jackie flies to my native island Corfu to attend Mass at the Church of Saint Francis and that when she receives Holy Communion she's not given the same wafers as ordinary mortals. Onassis had special ones made up for her—engraved with her initials!

In view of all this, it's a wonder they weren't able to get along better at the beginning of their marriage. The subject of their disputes seemed to vary from day to day. For example, Jackie couldn't get used to the way her husband appeared at meals. This may seem a minor matter, but for Jacqueline Bouvier there were certain rules of etiquette and good manners that could never be forgotten. She's in the habit of changing every night for dinner and gets annoyed when her husband stays in his shirt sleeves. Even when she comes home during the day she doesn't like to surprise him with his tie loosened and his shoes unlaced. Admittedly, even when they're invited out to dinner or eating in a restaurant, Onassis likes to undo his tie and discreetly take off his shoes.

But the way Onassis dresses for meals isn't half as aggravating to Jackie as the very loud noises he makes when he eats. I've often noticed that he can be heard from quite a distance, and when there's soup on the menu, it's positively disastrous. He breathes in with such gusto it's a wonder he doesn't swallow the spoon as well.

All of this just goes to show that these two people lead very separate lives, going about their own business without paying much attention to each other. For example, Onassis is a very active man and can hardly sit still five minutes in a row, while Jackie likes to lie around, reading and absorbing the sun. She often spends whole days in bed just because she feels a little tired or because she's going out that evening and wants to present a serene countenance to the world. Sometimes she remains closeted in her room for eight hours straight, wearing a beauty mask. And when she doesn't have her hairdresser with her, she actually sleeps sitting up in bed in order not to spoil her hairdo.

Onassis for his part often eats without his wife because he wants to hear some Greek music and amuse himself at Zampétas. Other times he goes over to Glyfada to dine with the Garoufalideses, or maybe he'll just take a boat over to Lefkas to eat his favorite foods, the grape leaves and goat cheese that Jackie so detests. Meanwhile, Jackie remains on the island or aboard the *Christina,* where she watches films while smoking tiny leather-covered pipes of different colors.

Naturally, Onassis was hoping for a much happier marriage, even though he must have been aware that he wasn't marrying the most tractable woman in the world. George and Hélène both told me they've often seen their employer looking sad and worried when he's in Paris. One of his greatest pleasures when he's there, however, is his family of canaries. He always asks right away, "Are there any new babies?" And if there are, he smothers the parents with love and tenderness.

I was told of one incident that indicated rather clearly how depressed and disillusioned he was by the apparent failure of his marriage. Because Onassis only spends a few days out of each month in Paris, George really has very little to do most of the time. As a result, he developed the hobby of building model houses. One day, returning from a long trip, Onassis found the latest masterpiece set out on the table. He looked at it long and hard before remarking sadly, "Your house is beautiful and well built. How lucky you are and how happy it must make you to be able to amuse yourself like that."

There's no doubt that by 1970, Onassis had decided to get a divorce. The following scene, which I heard about from a reliable source (one of Onassis' few confidants, in fact), took place in the library of Jackie's New York apartment. Onassis simply told her one evening that he couldn't continue to live this way any longer, that he would honor his marriage contract, but that he thought their marriage was a total failure; it would be better for them to separate. The two of them had no interests or tastes in common to fall back on. Since their marriage, they both continued to live more or less as they had when single. They hadn't really made a concentrated effort to create a solid bond that might possibly have helped them through this crisis.

Standing very straight in a yellow evening gown, Jackie seemed to accept her husband's decision without complaint. She replied that all further communication would be conducted through their lawyers. Onassis left the apartment for the Pierre, where he'd spent almost every night in New York since the marriage, and the next day, Friday, he took a plane to Paris. On Saturday, he could be seen dining at Maxim's with Maria Callas. There was even a photograph of them published in the newspapers, chatting comfortably after dinner over a bottle of champagne.

Perhaps this very photograph is what saved the situation. No one will ever know. It's certain, however, that Jackie flew to Paris the following Monday and arrived at his apartment around four o'clock in the afternoon. She came from the airport in a taxi, without a single bodyguard to protect her. She looked exhausted and when she took off her sunglasses her eyes were red and swollen from crying.

When she was informed that her husband was out, she calmly sat down to wait, and absently looked through magazines for the rest of the afternoon. When Onassis came home it was about 8:30 P.M. Jackie got up, very pale, took a few steps toward him, then threw herself into his arms and burst into tears. With this one gesture, she opened the door to a whole new life for them.

All their past resentment seemed to melt away and nothing else mattered. For the first time in years she had come down from her pedestal and acted like a wife who was in love with her husband. And the truth turns out to be that simple: Jackie really loves him. The moment he decided that everything was over between them, she realized that she was deeply in love with this self-made man who was admittedly a little rough in his ways, but was also the most unusual individual she'd ever encountered in her life.

In the next few months, they dumbfounded all those who had sworn that the marriage was a failure. Today, they're completely content with each other. Tomorrow? I have a strong feeling that tomorrow will find them much the same.

During the three days they spent in Paris before leaving for New York, they made a number of decisions, the most important of which was to take a second honeymoon, to last no less than a full year. And finally, at the age of sixty-five, the great businessman decided that it was time to stop working so hard. If his wife was prepared to give up some of her whims as a sacrifice to him, he could, for his part, make a concerted effort not to spend all of his waking hours at work.

A chance presented itself at just about this time. Onassis was supposed to negotiate a contract with the Greek government involving an investment of $600,-000,000 for the construction of an oil refinery in Piraeus. This deal could have doubled his fortune. But for the first time in his life he decided to let the opportunity go in order to avoid the increased pressure and work. Instead, he spent the time teaching his son Alexandre the intricacies of running his enormous business empire. When he was convinced that Alexandre was able to make most major decisions on his own, he set off for Greece with Jackie, beginning a long vacation.

After traveling on land for a few days, they returned to the *Christina* to take a short cruise in the Aegean. The entire crew immediately noticed the great change in their mistress. She no longer had her bodyguards and she smiled and spoke warmly to everyone. But most remarkable of all, she welcomed every opportunity to learn a few words of Greek, something she had completely neglected before, although her children already spoke it fluently.

Perhaps the most important change was in her behavior toward her husband. She made every effort to be an obedient and docile wife at all times. The widow of John Kennedy, who had made a marriage of convenience, gradually disappeared and the real Mrs. Onassis took her place once and for all.

I've already mentioned how Onassis is in the habit of going out two or three times a week when he's in Greece, either to call on his old friends or listen to music in one of his favorite nightclubs. Until now, Jackie always found these amusements too common for her and preferred to have her husband go out alone, even if it was only to Nikos' restaurant on Lefkas. This was a simple place where the fishermen of the region sat together at long, narrow tables and drank ouzo and ate Greek specialties. During her two years of marriage, Jackie had never once eaten there. But one night in January, 1971, alone and bored on the *Christina,* she asked to be taken there, where she knew her husband was having dinner. She found him in shirt sleeves, surrounded by a group of local fishermen. When she arrived, Onassis stood up proudly and had her sit next to him in the place of honor. Here, for the first time in her life, Jackie ate an entire Greek meal. What's more, she had such a good time that she sneaked back the next day in secret and spent the entire afternoon with Nikos' sister, learning how to make stuffed grape leaves.

At dinner, she happily presented her husband with the fruits of her labors. And she went back every day for three weeks to continue her course in Greek cooking. Her interest in Greek cuisine even led her—this woman who only a short while before hadn't been able to find the galley on her own yacht—to delight in watching the cooks and chatting about what they were making for dinner.

In February, Onassis asked his pilot to take him to Glyfada in the hydroplane so he could go to Zampétas. Jackie announced that she was coming with him. At about midnight, when the place was jammed with people, Onassis got up to dance. He didn't ask his wife to join him since he knew she didn't like to make herself conspicuous in that kind of place. But he had barely collected a group of people out on the floor before Jackie joined them. She danced nonstop for forty-five minutes. Onassis was so pleased to see his wife dancing to the native rhythms that he handed out one-hundred-dollar bills to everyone present, even to a photographer whom he had told not to take pictures. Despite this warning, the fellow couldn't resist taking advantage of this extraordinary occasion. But he only had time to flash two or three shots before Onassis, in a fit of sudden rage, picked up a chair and hurled it at him. When the young man started to fight back, it was the signal for a general brawl.

Jackie joined in too, coming to the rescue of her husband with her shoe, which she wielded with great force against anyone who dared attack him.

Finally, only a few minutes before the arrival of the police, Jackie and her husband escaped through the back door with their clothes in shreds and roared off in their car. Having blown her cool completely, Jackie abandoned herself to laughter while nestling against Ari, who for his part was only able to smile as he caught his breath. The evening cost them three thousand dollars, but Jackie swore she had never had such a good time in her life.

There were many more astonishing changes in this remarkable woman. Although she had always stayed away from Skorpios as much as possible because of her fear of earthquakes, she now took up gardening. She had plants flown over specially from Florida when she redesigned the flower beds. What's more, she went out every morning to pick bouquets of roses, tulips and orchids to fill the many vases in the three houses and the yacht.

But perhaps the most dramatic and meaningful transformation in the life of this extraordinary couple took place in March, 1971, while they were on a cruise. An unexpected storm hit the *Christina*. It frightened Jackie so much that around two in the morning she decided to wake her husband, who still slept below in the cabin Lesbos. She begged him to join her upstairs. On all subsequent nights, using the excuse that there could be another such storm at any moment, Jackie asked her husband to stay with her. This was the end of Clause Nineteen in the marriage contract. Since that time, whenever Onassis isn't away on business—and he's home more and more these days—he shares his wife's bed.

Everyone also noticed that Jackie, who always used to get more presents from Onassis than she ever gave in return, now made an effort to think of him far more than herself. When she goes shopping, she tries to come back with surprises for him. On Capri in April, she bought him three hundred sixty-five neckties, since she decided that his navy-blue and black ties were much too somber. Another time, in Miami, she bought him a cigar cutter of solid gold. She also started to paint portraits of him, which she hung all over the yacht.

Onassis, as usual, remembers his wife in very special ways. On the feast of Saint Jacqueline, very early in the morning, he mobilized an entire army of gardeners to gather all the most beautiful red roses on the island. He had the flowers loaded on a helicopter, then climbed in himself, next to the pilot. About nine o'clock, when

Jackie got up, they flew over her house and literally rained roses on her. A few hours later, over lunch, he presented her with a sculpture from Tiffany's depicting two children (John-John and Caroline) tenderly holding hands. And a few hours after that, they were off on yet another cruise, the fourth since the beginning of the year.

During this period of extended honeymoon for the newly reunited couple, the natives around Skorpios have gotten into the habit of coming over to the island in the evenings. They look for places where the two lovers might have expressed their passion, so they can make love there, hoping that the child which could come of it would be as beautiful as Jackie, as rich as Ari, and as happy as the Onassises.